This book may be kept

FOURTEEN DAYS

A fine will be charged for each day the book is kept overtime.

JAN 28 80			
GAYLORD 142			PRINTED IN U.S.A.

The Ecological Theater and the Evolutionary Play

Frontispiece. Painting, probably representing "Vision" in a series of the "Five senses," signed "J. V. Kessel fecit anno 1660." Pitti Palace, Florence

G. E. HUTCHINSON

The Ecological Theater

and the Evolutionary Play

NEW HAVEN AND LONDON:

YALE UNIVERSITY PRESS

Copyright © 1965 by Yale University.
Third printing, December 1969.
Designed by Sally Sullivan,
set in Baskerville type,
and printed in the United States of America by
The Carl Purington Rollins Printing-Office
of the Yale University Press.

Library of Congress catalog card number: 65–22321
Distributed in Great Britain, Europe, Asia,
and Africa by Yale University Press Ltd.,
London; in Canada by McGill-Queen's University
Press, Montreal; and in Mexico by Centro
Interamericano de Libros Académicos,
Mexico City.

34,969

For Ruth and Charles

Preface

The first three essays, grouped together, were delivered, in a slightly shorter form, as lectures at Temple University in Philadelphia in October 1964. "The Naturalist as Art Critic" was a lecture given at the annual meeting of the Academy of Natural Sciences of Philadelphia in 1963, at the close of the Academy's sesquicentennial year, and is reprinted with their permission. "The Lacustrine Microcosm Reconsidered" was an address given at the opening of the new Limnological Laboratory of the University of Wisconsin on Lake Mendota, and first appeared in print in the *American Scientist;* the final piece, which also was published in the *American Scientist,* represents a small historical study on the circumstances of a major biological discovery early in the present century. I am indebted to the Society of Sigma Xi for permission to reprint both pieces. The work leading to the last piece was done mainly in the Insect Rooms of the Museum of Zoology, University of Cambridge. I take particular pleasure in being able to associate in this book Philadelphia and Madison with Cambridge as centers of learning, which, though very different, have meant a great deal to me and my work.

I am much indebted to Temple University, the Academy of Natural Sciences of Philadelphia, and the University of Wisconsin for their invitations. The kindnesses of many friends in Philadelphia are too numerous to catalogue and too subtle to isolate, ranging continuously from fascinating exposition of biological theory to the opportunity to enjoy magnificent and often unexpected paintings; one very special indebtedness is indicated on another page. To Arthur D. Hasler of the University of Wisconsin I want to express my appreciation and thanks for the characteristic blend of limnology and music that I have enjoyed whenever visiting Madison. To John Smart of Cambridge I am deeply grateful for letting me have, in 1963, free access to the collections and books which had, forty years earlier, when they were under the care of my old friend the late Hugh Scott, F.R.S., provided such a stimulus, in directions that I then could not have suspected would lead to the concept of the multidimensional niche. I would also express my thanks to W. E. China of the British Museum (Natural History), the most helpful as well as the greatest living authority on the Hemiptera, for illustrative material and perennial past opportunities for study of the specimens under his care. I would also like to thank Charles L. Remington for making available the riches of the collection of Lepidoptera in the Peabody Museum of Yale University and likewise Percy A. Morris for many kindnesses that I have received in his beautiful shell room in the same museum. Where birds fly or rhinoceroses lumber into the text as examples, the learned will note the beneficent influence of S. Dillon Ripley. Conversations about *Conus* with Alan J. Kohn have been most illuminating. Since much of the book is in essence a set of variations on a theme by David Lack, F.R.S., I am particularly grateful to him for reading the whole work in proof.

In the preparation of the third lecture, concerning human evolution, I have had the opportunity of using some of Ursula Cowgill's partly unpublished demographic investigations, for which I am most grateful. I have also had the benefit of discussion with the remarkable group of investigators of the lower primates, Richard J. Andrew, John Buettner-Janusch, Alison Jolly, and Elwyn Simons, that was working so effectively at Yale during a large part of the past decade. Much of the matter in the third lecture grew out of such conversations, particularly with Alison Jolly. Conversations in Florence and Siena with René Dubos have taught me much. A number of additional and specific acknowledgments for help, information, and illustrations are given in the notes following each piece; such notes are purposefully extensive, so as to preserve something of the flavor of oral delivery, unhampered by elaborate detailed references, in the main body of the text. There is some overlap between the first and third contributions which has been retained, as to remove it would have destroyed the continuity of the Madison lecture.

In addition to the specific acknowledgments, my debt to my wife during the preparation of the book is particularly great.

G. E. H.

New Haven, Connecticut
December 1964

Contents

Illustrations

The Ecological Theater and the Evolutionary Play

I

The Biosphere or Volume in Which Organisms Actually Live

The part of the planet in which organisms live is usually called the biosphere.[1] Regarded from a cosmic point of view it is a rather peculiar region, though we may suspect that a very large class of biospheres exists on other planets throughout our galaxy and beyond.[2]

1. E. Suess, discussing the envelopes of the earth in the last and most general chapter of *Die Entstehung der Alpen* (Vienna, 1875), wrote (p. 159) of "eine selbständige Biosphäre." No note or other remark implies an earlier use of the term. W. I. Vernadsky, however, in the first note of what was probably his last publication (*Amer. Sci.*, *33*:1–12, 1945) implies that Lamarck had originated the term. It however does not seem to be used in J. B. Lamarck, *Hydrogéologie, ou Recherches sur l'influence qu'ont les eaux sur la surface du globe terrestre; sur les causes de l'existence du bassin des mers, de son déplacement et de son transport successif sur les différents points de la surface de ce globe; surfin sur les changements que les corps vivants exercent sur la nature et l'état de cette surface* (Paris, An X [i.e. 1802]). This work, however, must be regarded as one of the foundations of biogeochemistry; the arguments of the fourth chapter are very reminiscent of much of Vernadsky's own writings. Lamarck's chemistry was old-fashioned for his day but some of his intuitions are startling. He believed clays depended on the plant cover for their formation and that granites were essentially metamorphosed clays and not primary rocks.

2. See for instance Harrison Brown, Planetary systems associated with main-sequence stars, *Science*, *145*:1177–81, 1964. His numerical arguments

The biosphere, its nature and structure

The empirical extent of the biosphere as a natural region, that is to say as unextended by advanced human technology, reaches from very high on the highest mountains to the greatest depths of the ocean or probably more correctly a little way into the deepest ocean sediments. On land the biosphere penetrates to various depths in caverns and apparently also in very minute cracks and channels in which water may percolate and in which bacteria and animals may be found.

It is convenient to distinguish an active *eubiosphere* in which the physiological functions of organisms are possible, surrounded by a *parabiosphere* in general too hot, too cold, or too dry to permit any active metabolism but in which spores or other resting stages may exist. Most of the Antarctic and Greenland ice sheets, some local deserts, and the uppermost parts of the troposphere, in which spores but no other organisms occur, belong to this inactive part. The tops of the highest mountains may also belong here, though there is a record[3] of the bar-headed goose *Anser indicus* flying over the top of Mount Everest, and so at an altitude of about 9,000 m. and at an atmospheric pressure of about one-third that at sea level.

Within the eubiosphere two conditions are ordinarily met. The temperature is always near enough to that at which water is a liquid, so that within active organisms aqueous solutions can be present in a liquid state. There is also always, at some

---

have apparently failed to carry conviction with some other investigators, but even if his conclusions imply an abundance of habitable plants several magnitudes too great, there will still be a fantastic number in the galaxy.

3. George Lowe, in L. W. Swan, The ecology of the high Himalaya, *Sci. Amer.*, *205*:68–78, Oct. 1961. Dr. Swan most kindly informs me that soil and snow collected in sterile vials at altitudes between 25,000 and 27,500 feet (= 7,600–8,300 m.) have yielded on culture at least nine kinds of generically determinable microorganisms, and that it is reasonably certain that such organisms are metabolically active when the sun shines.

time in the year, either a radiation flux from the sun, which can be tapped by photosynthetic organisms, or a supply of photosynthetic products, which can be made available by the force of gravity or through transport by wind and water in regions that are inhabitable but lack autotrophic plants.

The two conditions of a liquid and an energy source are presumably fundamental. It is almost impossible to imagine anything like an organism developing as a pattern in a gaseous mixture, and though an adult completely solid-state organism might be thought of, it is difficult to conceive how it could develop. It is also important to note that although organisms can live in the free liquid phase of lakes and oceans, most species prefer an environment of interfaces; this may well have been a primitive preference.

Some energy source and sink are clearly needed if organisms are to function. Whenever the liquid water requirement can be met it is likely that the planet would be at the right distance from its sun star for the latter to be the obvious source of energy. The internal heat of a planet, mostly of radioactive origin, in theory would provide an alternative to incoming radiation though we have little precedent as to how an organism could use it. In considering some of the evidence of former extraterrestrial life the possibility of such endogenous energy stored as an unstable mixture of inorganic minerals has perhaps to be considered. Within the region of the eubiosphere we may distinguish between an *autobiosphere* in which the external energy source is trapped and converted into the chemical energy of organic compounds, today exclusively by the photosynthetic activity of chlorophyll-bearing plants, and two regions together forming the *allobiosphere* in which animals, heterotrophic plants, and bacteria can live, but into which organic food materials must be transported, ordinarily by gravity or by wind.

In the greatest depths of the ocean, as elsewhere below the euphotic zone, the food supply must consist ultimately of dead organisms, of feces and other detached, secreted, or excreted parts of organisms, and of particulate organic matter, in part originally in solution, and deposited on bubbles and other surfaces, including those of the organic particles themselves, which may apparently grow by accretion.[4] With all such sedimenting organic matter, bacteria are presumably usually associated. In the hypogean parts of the lower or *hypoallobiosphere,* the main sources of food are organic particles washed down by groundwater.

In the upper or *hyperallobiosphere* the nutrition is more precarious. At least in the vicinity of Mount Everest, sporadic flowering plants occur over 6,000 m. (*Stellaria decumbens* 6,136 m., *Arenaria muscosa* 6,218 m., and on Kangchenjunga *Delphinium glaciale* at 6,200 m.), but in a large part of the Himalaya and connected ranges much of the area over 5,500 m. is bare and constitutes an aeolian or supra-alpine zone[5] in

4. G. A. Riley, Organic aggregates in sea-water and the dynamics of their formation and utilization, *Limnol. Oceanogr., 8:*372–81, 1963; W. H. Sutcliffe, E. R. Baylor, and D. W. Menzel, Sea surface chemistry and Langmuir circulation, *Deep-Sea Res., 10:*233–43, 1963; G. A. Riley, P. Wangersky, and D. van Hemert, Organic aggregations in tropical and subtropical waters of the North Atlantic Ocean, *Limnol. Oceanogr., 9:*546–50, 1964.

5. The terms *aeolian* or *supra-alpine* zone are due to Swan (above, n. 3) in his most interesting general account of this remarkable region. He has discussed the matter further in Ecology of the heights, *Natural History Magazine,* April 1963, pp. 23–29, and in Aeolian zone, *Science, 140:*77–78, 1963.

E. Handschin's observations on Collembola living on snow fields in the Alps, feeding on windblown pollen, are fundamental. See his *Beiträge zur Kenntnis der wirbellosen terrestrischen Nivalfauna der Schweizerischen Hochgebirge* (dissertation, Basle, 1919); and also R. Hesse, W. C. Allee, and K. P. Schmidt, *Ecological Animal Geography* (New York and London, 1937), p. 498. Hutchinson (*The Clear Mirror,* Cambridge, 1937, partly reprinted as Lakes in the desert, *Amer. Sci., 37:*384–409, 1949) gave a brief general account in which the possible significance of insects flying upward but near the ground as a source of food for carnivores, in addition to the animals indigenous to the aeolian zone and feeding on windborne detritus, was considered. These ideas were partly derived from Hugh Scott, *Sirex gigas, Gastrophilus equi* and other insects on bare mountain-tops. *Entom. Month. Mag., 62:*19–20, 1926. Swan rightly calls attention to the organic matter in

which autotrophic organisms are absent. A limited but highly characteristic fauna penetrates considerably higher than do the autotrophic plants. This fauna consists mainly of springtails, mites, salticid spiders, and a few winged insects. On Everest salticid spiders appear to reach 6,700 m. The aeolian zone between 5,500 m. and 6,200 m. in the vicinity of this mountain has been well studied by Swan; all animals except the spiders and carnivorous mites must feed on windblown detritus, largely pollen grains but also other minute fragments of vegetation which can be observed on the stones of talus slopes well above

---

atmospheric precipitation, derived from soil and the sea surface, and certainly windborne, though in part at least in solution, as a further contribution. The most elevated record for terrestrial invertebrates remains that of Hingston (Life at high altitudes, *Geogr. Journ., 65*:185–98, 1925) for salticid spiders at 6,700 m. on Mount Everest. Swan's ecological observations presumably apply to the same species, but its exact determination remains to be published. The taxonomy of the fauna of the aeolian zone still is in fact quite inadequately known. Denis (*Mem. Conn. Acad. Sci., 10*:261–82, 1936) has recorded, from 5,300 to 5,600 m. from talus strewn or stony ground at or a little above the local limit of vegetation, five species of springtail, namely *Friesea excelsa* Denis, *Isotoma spinicauda* Bonet, *Orchesellides* cf. *boraoi* Bonet, *Entomobrya* (now *Mydonius*) *hutchinsoni* Denis, and *M.* cf. *lanuginosa* (Nic.), any of which may be expected to penetrate well into the aeolian zone in the Himalaya and connected regions. Birds feeding on insects may perhaps breed up to 6,440 m. (the wall creeper *Tichodroma muraria nepalensis;* see R. Meinertzhagen, Ladakh with special reference to its natural history, *Geogr. Journ., 70*:129–56; cf. Swan [above, n. 3]); among mammals, the pika *Ochotona ladakensis* occurs just under 6,000 m., and such levels may also be visited by the bharal *Pseudois nayaur,* which has an extraordinary capacity to run at these great altitudes. Reptiles, the least expected group of terrestrial animals to occur high on mountains, are known (*Leiolopisma ladacensis* [see Swan, The herpetology of Nepal, *Proc. Calif. Acad. Sci.,* 4th ser., *32*:103–47, 1962]) up to 5,500 m.

The upper limit of phanerogamic vegetation (see A. W. Hill, discussion in *Geogr. Journ., 65*:195–97, 1925), usually a little under 6,000 m., is, as both Hutchinson and Swan indicate, determined in part by availability of water. L. R. Wager, however (List of plants collected in the Rongbuk Valley, contributed to H. Ruttledge, *Everest 1933* [London, 1934]) suggests that low atmospheric pressure, which would lead to a partial pressure of CO_2 about half that at sea level, may contribute to the limitation. Since at the partial pressures prevalent in the atmosphere the photosynthetic activity of plants

the local limit of vegetation. Such fragments may well bear bacteria and fungi. The spiders and such carnivorous mites as are present would then have a supply of food in the springtails, mites, and flies. It is also conceivable that an additional source of food for carnivorous arthropods may exist on account of a tendency that can apparently be noticed in some insects, such as the small pierid butterfly *Baltia,* and quite likely widely distributed among several orders, of flying upward but at a rather small distance from the ground. This will cause the insects to ascend slopes and often to fly around pinnacles where they are trapped by such behavior. The matter clearly requires further study.

If we divorce ourselves from our biological knowledge and look at the biosphere as a mineralogist might see its contents, a number of the familiar concepts of natural history appear in a new light.[6]

---

is almost linearly dependent on the CO_2 pressure, a reduction of the latter, in a plant with an enforced short growing season, might be significant. It must however be remembered that the rate of respiration would be very low at night on account of the low temperature, and that this might compensate for low photosynthetic activity. The problem deserves further study.

The shortness of the growing season clearly limits the upward altitudinal extension of some groups, particularly of insects with an annual life cycle. The coldness of the nights at altitudes at which there is great radiative loss undoubtedly provides a more severe limitation than in localities having comparable daytime temperatures in the arctic. Aquatic Heteroptera reaching about 4,580 m. provide an example (T. Jaczewski, On two species of Corixidae from the Himalayas, *Ann. Mag. Nat. Hist.,* ser. 10, *12:*588–91, 1933; Hutchinson, A revision of the Corixidae of the Indian Empire, *Trans. Conn. Acad. Arts Sci., 33:*339–476, 1940). In the terrestrial Heteroptera, the highest record refers to a species, *Tibetocoris margaretae,* occurring on *Artemisia minor* but not living on the rather small specimens of the plant at the upper edge of the latter's range (Hutchinson, Lakes in the desert [above, n. 5]). In one or two cases, notably those of aquatic mollusks or of charophytes, the highest recorded specimens appear to come from warm springs. Evidently, in different groups with different types of life history, very different factors control the upper limits of occurrence.

6. W. I. Vernadsky dealt with this type of approach at considerable length; his ideas are accessible to the English reader in Problems of bio-

The region is of course a very active one, if only because it is the inner part of the terrestrial envelope to receive solar radiation. As a result of this activity, much of which involves biochemical processes, a large number of compounds or classes of compounds occur in the biosphere which are rare or unknown elsewhere. Some of these are organic compounds, which when they occur today outside organisms are usually stable, highly polymerized, and chemically difficult materials like humic acids, though a few simple organic minerals, notably oxalates, are known. There are also all the hydrated layer-lattice silicates, doubtless produced inorganically but mainly in regions in which biological processes actively occur. The organisms living within the biosphere, however, provide its most peculiar contents.

From the mineralogical point of view living organisms consist of classes of similar-looking bodies or species, each class having a characteristic size range and each member of which consists of an enormous number of different compounds of varying molecular weight. Although the proportions of the elements in the mixture have no stoichiometric significance, the actual elementary composition may be at least as constant, often more so, than that of a mineral to which a definite lattice structure can be assigned. Moreover there are enough differences between species in some genera for the elementary composition to be a specific character.

From a deeper molecular point of view any organism in its phenotypic expression is the projection into the macroscopic world of a most complex microscopic molecular pattern. This, coupled with the property of self-duplication, often gives the members of a biological species a much greater unity than the pebbles in a stream bed, or any other comparable macroscopic

---

geochemistry II, The fundamental matter-energy difference between the living and inert natural bodies of the biosphere, *Trans. Conn. Acad. Arts Sci.*, 35:483–517, 1944; and The biosphere and the noösphere, *Amer. Sci.*, 33:1–12, 1945.

collection of objects in nature. One only has to compare the members of a flock of juncos, on the one hand, and the stones in an open field where they are feeding, on the other, to see this. It is interesting to try to devise operational definitions of organisms in which there is no classificatory term such as "is a member of the same species" or "has an equivalent structure" or the like. It will soon be found that most organisms in the biosphere could not be recognized as such without terms of this kind and the concepts that they mean, for neither a reproductive nor a metabolic criterion is of any practical significance unless it can be transferred from individual to individual without making a new observation or experiment every time. Given the applicability of a classificatory process, observations are sufficiently numerous to suggest the induction that any member of a set of organisms having equivalent structure has arisen from some other member of the set. For any given set, except man and some domestic animals, this conclusion, the principle of abiogenesis as it has been called, has been verified in a very small proportion of cases. As it stands it is undoubtedly true, but the fact that any member of a species has had at least one parent also of that species does not mean that species do not change or that life could not originate on earth.

Reduced and oxidized parts of the biosphere

Apart from the temperature limits needed to have liquid water, and the requirement of an energy source, there is probably one important general chemical condition that must be met if a body of condensed cosmic matter is to develop a biosphere.

There is every reason to believe that the earth's atmosphere and hydrosphere are almost entirely secondary.[7] The very low

7. H. Brown, Rare gases and the formation of the earth's atmosphere, in *The Atmosphere of the Earth and Planets,* ed. G. P. Kuiper (2d ed. Chicago, 1952), pp. 258–66.

terrestrial proportion of the cosmically abundant gas neon, which has almost the same molecular weight as water (Ne 21, H_2O 18), indicates that the latter compound entered the earth originally in a solid form as ice or as water of hydration, and that initially the bodies forming the protoplanet were too small to hold any significant amount of the lighter, and actually also practically none of the heavier, permanent gases. This meant an enormous loss of atmophil elements, notably hydrogen, though doubtless carbon (CH_4 16, CO 28, CO_2 44, C_2N_2 56) and nitrogen (N_2 28, NH_3 17) as well. All three elements are however capable of being stored in a solid form, hydrogen as H_2O or –OH in the lattices of hydrated minerals, carbon as the free element, as carbides or possibly as carbonates, nitrogen as ammonium chloride or in smaller amounts as ammonium ions substituting for potassium in silicate rocks. Oxygen, being largely a lithophil element, would suffer a loss only as water or oxides of carbon. The result of the loss of the primary atmosphere thus makes the terrestrial planets of our system (Mercury, Venus, Earth, and Mars; our moon belongs in the same cosmochemical category) far less reduced bodies than the major planets which developed without losing most of their atmophil elements.

The terrestrial biosphere, therefore, although it may well originally have comprised a moderately reduced atmosphere lacking free oxygen, is not so overwhelmed with hydrogen as to be unable to develop great local differences in oxidation. It is by virtue of such differences that it works as an overall planetary mechanism. In its present state this is very easily apparent. Merely comparing the potential (about 0.0 to 0.1 volt relative to the standard hydrogen electrode) developed at a bright platinum electrode pushed into lake mud with the potential when the electrode is immersed in the surface waters of the lake (around 0.5 volt) gives a very simple demonstration of the division of the biosphere into regions which in theory could be developed to run an engine.

The most important and oldest type of division is doubtless that between the insides and outsides of the bodies of organisms. It has been apparent, from the very earliest development of steam engines, that such mechanisms could, and in fact often did, run on wood. This is in a simple diagrammatic form the process of utilizing the energy difference between the more reduced interior of the body of an organism and the exterior atmosphere, to obtain useful work.

The process in organisms is however molecular rather than macroscopic and of immense complexity. All that is needed ecologically is an external source of energy; physiologically all the rest can be imagined as occurring inside the organism, though ordinarily on earth material as well as energy passes in and out of the organism in metabolism.

The suggestions that are available about the origin of life and the existence of biospheres in other parts of the universe are of course speculative, but are definitely impressive. We know from the large number of experiments, initiated at various times during the past century but recently prosecuted with particular vigor as the result of Miller's well-known investigations,[8] that under the influence of various energy sources, such as an electric discharge or ultraviolet light, a great number of organic molecules, including amino acids and purines, can be synthesized[9] in models of prebiological atmospheres over an aqueous phase. There is also evidence[10] from the experiments

8. S. L. Miller, A production of amino acids under possible primitive earth conditions, *Science, 117*:528–29, 1953.

9. The best recent summary of the work that followed and was stimulated by Miller's experiments is given by J. Oro, Studies in experimental organic cosmochemistry, *Ann. New York Acad. Sci., 108*:464–81, 1963.

10. S. W. Fox, Evolution of protein molecules and thermal synthesis of biochemical substances, *Amer. Sci., 44*:347–59, 1956; S. W. Fox and S. Yugama, A biotic production of primitive protein and formed microparticles, *Ann. New York Acad. Sci., 108*:487–94, 1963; S. W. Fox, A theory of macromolecular and cellular origins, *Nature, 205*:328–40, 1965. In this paper definite comparison between Fox's synthetic microspheres and some of the bodies in carbonaceous chondrites are made.

of Fox that protenoid material might be synthesized from dry amino acids by polymerization at moderate temperatures around 170°C, though this mode of synthesis is perhaps not geochemically very attractive. The materials formed, however, when they come in contact with water produce populations of small spherical bodies, of standard size in any given experiment.

Carbonaceous chondrites

We have quite definite evidence from the study of one particular class of meteorites, the carbonaceous chondrites, that conditions, suggestive at least of prebiospheres, must have existed on or in nonterrestrial objects that formed part of the solar system early in its history.

The most important of the carbonaceous chondrites fell at Orgueil (Plate I) in southern France, just a century ago. Fragments were recovered almost immediately after its fall and it was early recognized as a most peculiar object. About 11.5 kg. of material collected in the neighborhood of the site are known and, although some specimens may have become contaminated at least superficially with dust and other substances in museums, there is every reason to suppose that most of its extraordinary chemical characters are inherent. The fact that a modern plant and a piece of coal were worked into one fragment just after the fall, probably as a hoax, does not apparently cast doubt on work done on other fragments.

The Orgueil stone consists of a mixture of materials, part of which must have formed at a high temperature,[11] but which in its final form must have been assembled in an aqueous medium at a low temperature, in a moderately reducing en-

11. E. R. DuFresne and E. Anders, Chemical evolution of the carbonaceous chondrites, in *The Solar System*, eds. B. M. Middlehurst and G. P. Kuiper, Vol. IV, *The Moon, Meteorites and Comets*, Chicago, 1963, pp. 496–526; E. Anders, On the origin of carbonaceous chondrites, *Ann. New York Acad. Sci., 108*:514–33, 1963.

vironment, containing carbon dioxide and sulfate but no free oxygen. A good deal of magnetite is present, apparently as an alteration product of olivine. In some of the other carbonaceous chondrites a less intense metamorphism seems to have produced a hydrated layer-lattice silicate. In the aqueous medium, calcium carbonate was deposited and later dolomitized, a process Anders thinks would have taken a time of the order of 10^3 years. Magnesium sulfate crystallized from the medium, forming a discrete vein of material. Elementary sulfur is also present. The quantity of carbon occurring in some sort of organic combination appears to be about 1 per cent of the mass of the stone. If the class of carbonaceous chondrites comprises about 0.1 to 1.0 per cent of the total mass of meteorites, as is reasonable, the overall organic content of meteorites is of the order of 1 in 10^4 to 10^5, greater than it would be for the earth as a whole, a rather surprising conclusion.[12] Apart from highly polymerized dark material the main organic compounds appear to be hydrocarbons, but carboxylic acids also are present in small amounts.[13] Adenine and guanidine derivatives certainly occur, as do considerable amounts of melamine and ammeline. The latter two compounds have a symmetrical triazine ring, in which three carbon and three nitrogen atoms alternate. Such structures are not known in biologically significant compounds but could probably be easily produced in an environment comparable to that in which other simple organic compounds form.[14] Tetrapyrrole compounds probably occur as vanadyl porphyrins, as in old terrestrial sediments.[15] Material extracted with a benzol-methanol

12. C. Sagan, Exobiology: a critical review, Fourth International Space Science Symposium (COSPAR), Warsaw, Poland, June 1963, mimeo. preprint, 35 pp.

13. B. Nagy, M. J. J. Murphy, V. E. Modzeleski, G. Rouser, G. Claus, D. J. Hennessy, U. Colombo, and F. Gazzarrini, Optical activity of saponified organic matter isolated from the Orgueil meteorite, *Nature*, *202*:228–33, 1964.

14. R. Hayatsu, Orgueil meteorite: Organic nitrogen content, *Science*, *146*:1291–92, 1964.

15. G. W. Hodgson and B. L. Baker, Evidence for porphyrins in the Orgueil meteorite, *Nature*, *202*:125–31, 1964. G. Mueller, "Impact contami-

mixture appears to show, when saponified, a very weak levo-rotatory optical activity, not due to amino acids. A variety of control materials, notably soil, pollen, and museum dust, extracted in the same way, gave either dextrorotatory activity or were inactive. The optically active material appears therefore to be a genuine extraterrestrial constituent, which suggests a biological as well as a prebiological history for the object before its arrival on earth. It must however be emphasized that other organic compounds with asymmetrical carbon atoms present in the meteorite appear not to exhibit optical activity.

A number of supposedly organized bodies, claimed to be fossils, have been identified. In general those that show least structure are best established as belonging in the meteorite; the more elaborate objects recorded are almost certainly terrestrial pollen grains and comparable contaminants. However when the size frequency[16] of the common autochthonous bodies is plotted, there is evidence of a multimodal distribution that is hard to explain unless the bodies are fossils representing several species. They could, however, perhaps be mixtures of protenoid microspherules of different sizes formed under different conditions, as in Fox's experiments, and later fossilized by replacement.

It is most curious that the sulfate in Orgueil is depleted in

---

nation" of the Mokoia carbonaceous chondrite, *Nature*, *204*:567, 1965, expresses some skepticism as to the validity of the evidence for porphyrins in Orgueil.

16. G. Claus and E. A. Suba-C., Organised element distribution in relation to size in the Orgueil meteorite, *Nature*, *204*:118–20, 1964. The earlier work on the supposed fossils is summarized in various papers in the *Ann. New York Acad. Sci.*, *108*, 1963. In general there are two points of view, that of Claus and Nagy strongly in favor of a biological interpretation and that of Anders skeptical of such. A tentative intermediate position seems indicated. The recent discovery that one fragment was tampered with, probably to ridicule Pasteur, by the insertion of coal and a flowering spike of *Juncus conglomeratus*, is discussed by E. Anders, E. R. DuFresne, R. Hayatsu, A. Cavaillé, A. DuFresne, and F. W. Fitch, Contaminated meteorite, *Science*, *146*:1157–61, 1964.

S^{34} relative to the elementary sulfur, though physical equilibrium, and the known processes of bacterial metabolism, would give the opposite effect, as is ordinarily observed in terrestrial material.[17]

The environment in which carbonaceous chondrites of the Orgueil type were formed has been discussed at length by the recent students of the meteorite. It appears to be reasonably certain that the final history of the material involved occurred in a neutral or alkaline aqueous medium, free from oxygen but containing oxyacid anions such as sulfate and carbonate. In the case of the Orgueil stone the environment is believed to have been alkaline (pH 8.0–10.0) and with a redox potential less than –0.2 volt.[18]

The nearest modern terrestrial analogue to such an environment would be in the mixolimnion of a meromictic saline lake rich in magnesium, but such a locality would be free of oxygen as a result of bacterial activity rather than as a primary characteristic. Modern highly reduced waters are often fairly rich in phosphate, at least in comparison with the very low concentrations present wherever ferric iron may be present. The occurrence of such phosphate, as well as of ferrous iron, would no doubt increase the variety and significance of prebiological reactions possible.[19] The main doubts about meteorites of the

17. E. Anders, On the origin of carbonaceous chondrites, *Ann. New York Acad. Sci., 108*:514–33, 1963.

18. DuFresne and Anders (above, n. 11); Anders (above, n. 11); B. Nagy, W. G. Meinschein, and D. J. Hennessy, Aqueous low temperature environment of the Orgueil meteorite parent body, *Ann. New York Acad. Sci., 108*:534–52, 1963.

19. Sagan in all his writings on the matter has emphasized the importance of the synthesis of adenosine triphosphate in the prebiosphere. Ultraviolet irradiation of mixtures of bases and sugars in the presence of phosphates in aqueous solution produces nucleosides and nucleoside phosphates, including adenosine triphosphate (C. Ponnamperuma, R. Mariner, and C. Sagan, Formation of adenosine by ultra-violet irradiation of a solution of adenine and ribose, *Nature, 198*:1199–1200, 1963). The importance of the reduced environment in permitting solution of phosphate in the presence of the normal geochemical excess of iron has not been adequately appreciated.

kind that is biologically interesting are the nature and size of the parent objects from which they are derived and whether the water involved was superficial or in cavities at such a depth that an external source of radiant energy could not provide the energy needed for the initial organic syntheses. Such hidden bodies of water would be the only kind possible on a small asteroid. The biological possibilities of such an environment have been explored theoretically by Anders,[20] who supposes that nonequilibrium mixtures of minerals formed in rapid cooling could provide energy to some kind of living matter evolving for a time, even though in the absence of an external energy source such living matter could have no future, save occasionally to be fossilized and to be studied by exobiologists on another planet. Like all contemporary science nonfiction, the idea must not be dismissed, though the reactions suggested are not very appealing.

Is there a biosphere on Mars?

It is worthwhile, with the possibilities suggested by experiments and meteorites in mind, to look closely, if briefly, at Mars. Four lines of evidence have suggested the possibility of Martian life. None are conclusive, but the concatenation of the four is at least more suggestive than some biologists seem to have believed.

1. There is a seasonal color change, darkening the darker areas on Mars at times when the nearer polar cap is melting and finally appearing 20° below the equator in the opposite hemisphere. Modern observers[21] record the changes as involving various shades of darkening gray, and such seasonal differences are easily seen on photographs (Plate I, *below*). The

---

20. Anders (above, n. 11).

21. For the older work consult E. M. Antoniadi, *La Planète Mars* (Paris, 1930); for a very good account of more recent observations see A. Dollfus, Visual and photographic studies of planets at the Pic du Midi, in *The Solar System,* eds. B. M. Middlehurst and G. P. Kuiper, vol. III, *Planets and Satellites* (Chicago, 1961), pp. 534–71.

earlier students recorded more dramatic color changes involving shades of green, blue, and even carmine. Some subjective errors are almost certainly involved, but it is possible that at present the changes are not as dramatic as they used to be early in the present century. These changes have been explained in terms of the hydration and dehydration of some mineral, but no compound of the common lithophil elements, which surely would be involved, has ever been suggested that would produce the observed effects within a reasonable range of vapor pressures. It has also been supposed that the alterations merely involve wetting the soil, but the amount of water available, the persistence of the changes, and the distances from the polar caps involved, seem to make this simple hypothesis very unlikely indeed.

2. The polarization of the light reflected[22] from both the bright desert areas and the dark areas in winter suggests reflection from particles about 0.1 mm. in diameter, but during the spring and early summer when the seasonal darkening occurs the areas exhibiting the change appear to be covered with progressively somewhat larger particles, as if something were swelling or growing. Dollfus, the chief investigator of the matter, suggests that the growth of unicellular algae would provide a suitable model.

3. The existence in the infrared reflection spectrum of the dark, but not of the light, areas of features between 3.4 and 3.7μ could be due to bonding in organic compounds.[23] Un-

22. A. Dollfus, Polarization studies of planets, ibid., pp. 343–99. R. Smoluchowski, Is there vegetation on Mars?, *Science, 148*:946–47, 1965 suggests that both the changes in color and polarization are due to photons and corpuscular matter from solar flares acting on rhyolite. The apparent seasonality is not explained.

23. W. M. Sinton, Spectrographic evidence for vegetation of Mars, *Astrophys. J., 126*:231–39, 1957; Further evidence of vegetation on Mars, *Science, 130*:1234, 1959; N. B. Colthrup, Identification of aldehyde in Mars vegetation regions, *Science, 134*:529, 1961. For a criticism, showing the lack of inevitability in the comparisons with terrestrial materials, see D. G. Rea, T. Belsky, and B. Calvin, Interpretation of the 3 to 4 micron infra-red

fortunately, however, the closest agreement of the bands at 3.54 and 3.77µ is with acetaldehyde, a volatile substance which would have to be rapidly produced and decomposed in rather large amounts to give an effect limited to the dark areas. The most recent study suggests that the observed bands are due to deuterium; if so, water must be continually evaporated from and condensed on the dark areas.

4. The rather high CO_2 content of the Martian atmosphere[24] corresponding to a partial pressure of 3 to 6 millibars, contrasted with the terrestrial content existing at the partial pressure of 0.3 millibar, suggests a nonequilibrium condition, since in reactions of the form

$$MSiO_3 + CO_2 \rightleftharpoons MCO_3 + SiO_2$$

the equilibrium value for the CO_2 pressure seems in general below that of the terrestrial partial pressure. The reactions involve water, and the establishment of equilibrium might be spotty and difficult in so dry a planet. Moreover it is conceivable that at the present time no undecomposed silicates are exposed to the atmosphere on Mars so that the reaction could not take place for lack of one of the major components. The most reasonable explanation of the observed CO_2 content is, however, that it represents a steady-state concentration in a biological cycle, as the smaller amount on earth also seems to do.

If these observations are taken to suggest life on Mars, there

----

spectrum of Mars, *Science, 141*:923–27, 1963; but compare also C. Sagan, Exobiology: a critical review, to appear in Fourth International Space Science Symposium (COSPAR), Warsaw, Poland, June 1963. Since the lecture was delivered, evidence that the bands are due to deuterium has been given by T. S. Shirk, W. A. Haseltine, and G. C. Pimental, Sinton bands: Evidence for deuterated water on Mars, *Science, 147*:48–49, 1965. D. G. Rea, B. T. O'Leary, and W. M. Sinton, Mars: the origin of the 3.58 and 3.69 micron minimum in the infra-red spectrum, *Science, 147*:1286–88, 1965, indeed suspect the bands originate in the Earth's atmosphere.

24. L. D. Kaplan, G. Münch, and H. Spinrad, An analysis of the spectrum of Mars, *Astrophys. J., 139*:1–15, 1964.

are still certain difficulties. The amount of water available is exceedingly small. The spectrographically detectible amount[25] in the atmosphere is 1.4 ± 0.7 mg. cm^{-2}. There is always some water present in one or other of the polar caps, and it is possible that there is a good deal of water that has been lost superficially in minerals at the Martian surface. Some may be present as permafrost, while the supposed organisms themselves, if they had an impermeable enough surface, might contain a quite appreciable amount of the total available water as a solution of some soluble salt or low molecular weight organic material, acting as an antifreeze, as glycerol does in insects. Magnesium nitrate with a eutectic temperature of $-29.0°C$ or calcium nitrate with one at $-28.8°C$ might be, in view of the next paragraph, possible constituents.

The absence of oxygen in the atmosphere suggests that if photosynthetic organisms occur, they do not produce free oxygen into the atmosphere. Sagan, Hanst, and Young[26] indicate that if any nitrogen oxides are present, that in greatest quantity would be NO. This could react with water to give nitrous acid, which would probably largely attack mineral matter forming nitrites. In terrestrial deserts there is a tendency for nitrate to accumulate; possibly, in the absence of O_2, but not under extreme reducing conditions, nitrite might form in the same way. At any rate there seems no clear reason why the loss of HNO_2 to the solid phase should be negligible. It has previously been suggested that a redox system involving NO_2 and NO_3 could well exist in Martian organisms, providing a sink for photosynthetic, and a source for respiratory, oxygen. The latter situation is common in bacteria that reduce nitrate in regions of low oxygen, but not too low redox, potential. The only further obvious requirement of a Martian organism is probably some protection against ultraviolet radiation, though the exact

25. Ibid.
26. C. Sagan, P. L. Hanst, and A. T. Young, Nitrogen oxides on Mars, mimeo. preprint, 31 + vi pp. (n.pl., n.d.).

extent of the need for this protection is uncertain. This might involve quite remarkable metabolic properties, particularly since in an organism 0.1 mm. across, a very thick opaque cuticle seems unlikely.

It is I think very clear that the concept of Martian organisms is far from impossible; it is indeed now known that terrestrial soil bacteria can survive synthetic Martian conditions.[27]

Stages in the history of the earth's biosphere

To return to the earth, its history, the stage for which we have been discussing, clearly involves a series of acts, about which we can say only a little, and for each one in widely disparate terms.

There is first the synthesis of a large number of organic molecules, probably all the building blocks that could be needed, and some irrelevant compounds like ammeline and melamine, in a moderately reducing aqueous medium at fairly low temperatures. This no doubt occurred at various places in the solar system, at least on earth and on or in the parent body of Orgueil, if not on Mars. The main processes involved can be studied as much as is desired in the laboratory. Much more work is clearly needed in which the results of the primary reactions in the gaseous phase can enter a hydrosphere of complicated but geochemically probable composition, since some essential step in prebiological synthesis may well depend on a minor constituent and quite surprising results might reward the investigator who used the right mixture. It is moreover worthwhile to consider, as Sagan has done,[28] the consequences of the decline in the rate of angular velocity of rotation of the earth due to tidal friction. If the initial velocity were several times that of today, not only would the photoperiod of ultraviolet light and the period of diurnal change of temperature be shortened,

27. S. Scher, E. Packner, and C. Sagan, to appear in Fourth International Space Science Symposium (COSPAR), Warsaw, Poland, June 1963.
28. C. Sagan, Radiation and the origin of the gene, *Evolution, 11*:40–55, 1957.

but the hydrosphere, even though it presumably consisted originally of relatively shallow bodies of water, might be divided even more than today into a very actively mixed upper zone with strong currents in which the probability of any small mass of water being exposed to ultraviolet for a time would be significant, and, at a moderate depth, water that remained relatively quiescent for months on end in a zone below that of ultraviolet penetration.

A laboratory model in which the gas and an agitated part of the aqueous phase were irradiated while diffusion into a dark and quiet part of the latter was possible might be worth considering.

Secondly, and perhaps we should say thirdly, fourthly, through an indefinite series of ordinal numbers, there occurred the polymerization of the results of the first act to give self-reproductive organisms capable of evolution by natural selection. The staggering complexity of these steps can be realized from what is now known about the structure of a single gene and about how it is likely to work. Although we now know in principle the kinds of processes that are involved in the essential nature of living matter, namely in its capacity for reproduction with inheritance, variation, and evolution on the nucleic acid side, and, rather more vaguely, in development and metabolism on the protein side, we can as yet form no real conception as to how the simplest imaginable organism could have developed from the prebiological organic soup. A large number of interesting suggestions have been made, but very few of them can be given any environmental reference. In view of Bernal's suggestion[29] that arrangement of organic molecules on the surface of an inorganic crystal lattice might produce initial structure, it seems worthwhile to suggest that the rather odd hydrated layer-lattice silicates of the carbonaceous chondrites deserve more study.

When the original evolving organisms were established, pre-

29. J. D. Bernal, *The Physical Basis of Life,* London, 1952.

sumably as heterotrophs, we were set for a new revolution, the production of photosynthetic oxygen and the development of the existing oxidized biosphere. From the standpoint of the present lecture this revolution marked the beginning of the modern world, though it was presumably a world not yet inhabited by eucaryote organisms with ordinary nuclei, mitochondria, and plastids. Though oxygen can be produced by processes such as the photolysis of water vapor, the arguments of Berkner and Marshall,[30] earlier made by Wildt for Mars, that this oxygen, present in small amounts, will be drawn off by oxidation of the superficial lithosphere, by ozone formed photochemically, seems valid. The modern atmosphere with its mixture of nitrogen, oxygen, and water vapor over liquid water, not in thermodynamic equilibrium, is clearly a consequence of the existence of living matter.

It is possible, as Sagan[31] and others have concluded, that prior to the evolution of ordinary photosynthesis, organisms were provided with a catalase system to detoxify peroxides formed by the action of ultraviolet light. The evolution of free oxygen may not have therefore been as devastating initially to anaerobic organisms as would otherwise have been the case. But by putting the older organisms, unable to engage in ordinary aerobic metabolism, at a great competitive disadvantage and by producing the ozone screen which cut off most of the ultraviolet that had formerly reached the base of the atmosphere and had been the primary energy source of organic synthesis, the evolution of oxygen must have been a catastrophic cause of extinction of the old anaerobic biota of the earth.

The possibility of the production of an oxidized surface without the accumulation of oxygen in the atmosphere makes

30. L. V. Berkner and L. C. Marshall, The history of oxygenic concentration in the earth's atmosphere, Southwestern Center for Advanced Study, mimeo., 68 pp.

31. C. Sagan, On the origin and planetary distribution of life, *Radiation Res.*, *15*:174–92, 1962; perhaps the most learned and exciting treatment of the theme yet to appear.

arguments from changes in the oxidation of pre-Cambrian sediments, stressed by several authors, somewhat uncertain. Rankama's observations[32] suggesting an oxygen-free atmosphere some time after 2.10^9 years ago are more critical than those of his predecessors and have a certain appeal, though some recent workers believe that photosynthetic oxygen was liberated much earlier. Berkner and Marshall's view that the appearance of a full fossil record with the opening of the Cambrian corresponds to the development of an atmosphere rich in oxygen, though unlikely to appeal to most biologists, deserves serious consideration.

The production of oxygen must presumably at first have concerned organisms referable to the photosynthetic procaryote Monera, and comparable to the modern blue-green algae. The oldest known[33] certain fossil organisms, from the Gunflint formation of southern Ontario, dated $1.9 \pm 0.2 \times 10^9$ years ago, consist of a rather diversified assemblage of largely filamentous forms. Though some were tentatively referred by Tyler and Barghoorn to the fungi, the small diameters of these fossils would not be inconsistent with all of them having been procaryote organisms belonging to the Monera. The same may well be true of the problematic objects described[34] from

32. K. Rankama, Geological evidence of chemical composition of the Precambrian atmosphere, *Geol. Soc. Amer. Special Paper, 62*:651–64, 1955; the best argument for a late date for the appearance of free oxygen. Sagan (above, n. 31) accepts the simple analytical evidence of highly oxidized iron in much older rocks as evidence for a relatively short period before photosynthetic oxygen appeared. The subject is likely to be restudied extensively. See also a symposium to appear in the *Proc. Nat. Acad. Sci.* during the summer of 1965.

33. S. A. Tyler and E. S. Barghoorn, Occurrence of structurally preserved plants in the pre-Cambrian rocks of the Canadian shield, *Science, 119*:606–08, 1954; E. S. Barghoorn and S. A. Tyler, Microorganisms from the Gunflint Chert, *Science, 147*:563–77, 1965. See also P. E. Cloud, *Science, 148*:27–35, 1965.

34. C. G. A. Marshall, J. W. May, and C. J. Perret, Fossil microorganisms: possible presence in pre-Cambrian shield of Western Australia, *Science, 144*:290–92, 1964.

Western Australia by Marshall, May, and Perret, which may not be fossils and may be, but by no means certainly are, 2.7×10^9 years old. Supposed algal concretions apparently without cellular remains are known[35] from Southern Rhodesia from limestone of about the same degree of antiquity, but neither occurrence can be accepted with anything like the confidence that may be placed in Tyler and Barghoorn's Gunflint material. *Corycium enigmaticum,* a macroscopic form up to 30 cm. long, from Finland,[36] apparently a little younger than the Gunflint, might be a large algal cell like that of the green alga *Hydrodictyon,* though much larger, but it has too few features to permit any certain judgment. Further material consisting of very broken fragments of cell walls, with organic compounds present, is known from about 1.1×10^9 years ago.[37] Of course at the present time we have no means of deciding if any of these organisms were photosynthetic.

The final act on the sort of scale we are considering begins with the opening of the Phanerozoic, the period in which there is at almost every time somewhere a rock being deposited in which recognizable fossils occur. Although the appearance of good fossils in the Cambrian is as dramatic an event as we can see in the geological record, a progress from penury to riches occurring at a fairly definite time about 6.10^8 years ago, it doubtless reflects something far less profound than the evolution of organic compounds, organisms, or the oxidizing atmosphere. There is still some doubt as to the oldest fossil animals. The fauna which probably gives the best hint as to what was going

35. A. M. Macgregor, A pre-Cambrian algal limestone in Southern Rhodesia, *Trans. Geol. Soc. S. Africa, 43:9–16,* 1940; see also L. H. Ahrens, Oldest rocks exposed, *Geol. Soc. Amer. Special Paper, 62:155–68,* 1955.

36. K. Rankama, New evidence of the origin of pre-Cambrian carbon, *Bull. Geol. Soc. Amer., 59:389–416,* 1948, gives an excellent account of *Corycium* with illustrations. Possible equivalent forms are indicated by B. L. Stinchcomb, H. L. Levin, and D. J. Echols, *Science, 148:75–76,* 1965.

37. W. G. Meinschein, E. S. Barghoorn, and J. W. Schopf, Biological remnants in a pre-Cambrian sediment, *Science, 145:262,* 1964.

on at the time of evolution of commonly fossilizable animals is certainly Ediacara in Southern Australia.[38] Though not all geologists believe that this fauna is really older than the conventional lower Cambrian, it seems to suggest what should precede the latter. For the most remarkable lower Cambrian animals are trilobites, and in the Ediacara fauna we have in *Spriggina* a worm-like organism originally placed improbably near the very specialized planktonic polychaete *Tomopteris*, but as Glaessner realized, surely much the kind of thing that might be expected to have been the annelid ancestor of trilobites and cephalocarid crustaceans. Between this type of organism and the minute and possibly procaryote organisms of the Gunflint, there is a vast period of more than a billion years in which not only perhaps the nucleus, but more certainly multicellularity, nervous systems, and behavior appeared. All the Ediacara organisms seem to have been shell-less and their fossilization due to an improbable chance. They well may show a fauna just before fossilizable shells became common, and again emphasize the question as to why fossils in several groups first occur when they do.

If we consider the fossil record provided by tracks, casts of burrows, impressions and rare actual preservation of organic materials, we have an extremely irregular sequence, beginning before the Cambrian, much enriched in the late Paleozoic by the abundant appearance of land plants, and demonstrating a few really dramatic and quite exceptional local events such as those leading to the fossilization of many soft-bodied animals in the Burgess Shale, and equally extraordinary occurrences in the Solenhofen formation. If we had no fossils based on skeletal structure, it is very unlikely that the concept of the Phanerozoic would have ever been developed. What are made apparent in the earliest Cambrian are not organisms so much as hard parts. With a record lacking skeletons of animals, the dramatic world-

38. M. F. Glaessner, New fossils from the base of the Cambrian South Australia, *Trans. R. Soc. S. Australia*, 81:185–88, 1958.

wide event of the Paleozoic would be the development of a terrestrial flora and not of a somewhat earlier marine fauna. In view of this and of the considerable period that would presumably be needed for the evolution of the eucaryote cell, multicellularity, the complexity of the bilateral nervous system and concomitant behavior, to name only the three most striking advances, any hypothesis involving major and catastrophic geochemical changes at the end of pre-Cambrian times seems rather improbable.

I still feel that the opinion put forward[39] for instance by H. K. Brooks and by myself in 1958, namely that the development of the fossilizable skeleton at the opening of the Phanerozoic reflects the initiation of predation, and that before this time the biosphere was largely a peaceable kingdom in which armor was not needed and therefore was not available as an epitaph, is the best explanation of the observed facts.

The paleontologically recognizable invertebrate phyla appear in the Cambrian; only the vertebrates, in which elaborate learned behavior finally became the dominant feature of life, seem to have originated within phanerozoid time, and of this we know almost nothing.

In looking at the Cambrian fossil record, the ecologist sees familiar problems, such as the existence of related sympatric species. At every stage in the evolutionary process the relationships of organism to environment have been doubtless complicated—how complicated will be apparent in the next lecture. An increase in complexity in the biological community as predation on animals as well as on plants develops would give

39. G. E. Hutchinson, The biologist poses some problems, in *Oceanography, Amer. Assoc. Adv. Sci.*, 1961, pp. 85–94. Brooks believed that the first predators were trilobites; Hutchinson, impressed by the fact that the known gnathobases of trilobites are well separated medially, considered nautiloid cephalopods or polychaete worms, organisms which, though then small, may have had quite powerful jaws, as the most likely primitive predators. Renewed consideration suggests that perhaps Brooks is more nearly right, though several forms may have been involved.

multilevel trophic communities, which, although they involve destruction of some animals, promote stability as they become more extensive. The pyramid of sizes and numbers is involved here; one way of avoiding being eaten is to be inconveniently large, and a way of avoiding not getting anything to eat is to be still larger. The drive toward size, which may of course get an animal nowhere, is however probably a necessary condition for development of a large nervous system. Animals cannot be all head and no body, though for a time, as the *Brontosaurus* suggests, they could be almost all body with very little head. The large nervous system involved in moving the muscles of a large animal also almost inevitably implies increase in number of connectible elements and so ultimately in learning ability. The overall relationship of an animal to what I would call the grain size or texture of its environment may be a fundamental condition for its ultimate evolutionary advance.

II

The Niche: An Abstractly Inhabited Hypervolume

In the previous lecture we examined the domain of life on earth, and speculated on possible domains elsewhere, largely in terms of transfer of energy and matter without saying much until the end about the individual organisms or kinds of organisms involved. This is a legitimate mode of abstraction, particularly when we know practically nothing about individuals or species, of a kind that I have elsewhere[1] called *hologi-cal,* since it relates to the properties of large units each treated as a whole. In the present lecture a much more *merological* approach will be attempted, though we shall still be concerned as much with unispecific populations as with individual orga-

1. G. E. Hutchinson, Food, time and culture, *Ann. New York Acad. Sci.,* ser. II, 5:152–54, 1943; The lacustrine microcosm reconsidered, *Amer. Sci.,* 52:334–41, 1964 (reprinted in this volume).

nisms. Various intermediate modes of approach can be formulated dealing hololologically with biological communities or, as in so much plant synecology, with parts of such communities. At the present time however these approaches, once they have provided the descriptive and classificatory schemes necessary to talk about the parts of communities and their changes in time, do not seem to have got very much further. The present attempt to say something about communities will begin primarily with species, considered as closely related but habitually noninterbreeding populations. This inquiry logically follows the final remarks of the previous lecture, for in the Lower Cambrian for the first time we have evidence not only of abundant and well-fossilized organisms but of closely related species living sympatrically. The ecology of species would seem a not unreasonable point of departure in an attempt to gain an understanding of some aspects of how biological communities are constructed.

Competitive exclusion

The fundamental starting point is actually what is best called the Principle of Competitive Exclusion,[2] which states that in equilibrium communities no two species occupy the same niche. The observational data suggesting some such principle to be generally operative were known to various late nineteenth- and early twentieth-century naturalists, notably Steere[3] and Grinnell.[4] The mathematical investigations of Haldane,[5] Volterra,[6]

2. G. Hardin, The competitive exclusion principle, *Science, 131:*1292–97, 1960.

3. J. B. Steere, On the distribution of genera and species of non-migratory land-birds in the Philippines, *Ibis*, 1894, pp. 411–20.

4. J. Grinnell, The origin and distribution of the chestnut-backed chickadee, *Auk, 21:*364–82, 1904.

5. J. B. S. Haldane, A mathematical theory of natural and artificial selection, *Trans. Cambridge Philos. Soc., 23:*19–41, 1924.

6. V. Volterra, Variazioni e fluttuazioni del numero d'individui in specie animali conviventi, *Mem. R. Acad. Naz. dei Lincei*, ser. 6, 2:31–113, 1926.

and Lotka[7] indicated that, provided certain axioms were satisfied, the principle inevitably followed for two species utilizing a common and not infinite resource, the rate of availability of which limited the size of the total population. The experiments of Gause[8] and his associates[9] and later of Park, Gregg, and Lutherman,[10] Park,[11] Crombie,[12] Frank,[13] and other investigators confirmed experimentally the essential conclusions of the mathematical theory. In such an experimental confirmation it is to be noted that what is being done is to set up populations of organisms under conditions which satisfy the postulates incorporated into the theory, so that the observed magnitudes of the populations provide numerical solutions, for various values of time, of the differential equations describing the processes of the growth or decline of these populations. In general the competing populations do not constitute very good analogue computers, but the theory in general, for in-

7. A. J. Lotka, The growth of mixed populations, two species competing for a common food supply, *J. Wash. Acad. Sci.*, *22*:461–69, 1932.

8. G. F. Gause, *The Struggle for Existence*, Baltimore, 1934; Vérifications expérimentales de la théorie mathématique de la lutte pour la vie, *Actual. scient. indust.*, no. 277, Paris, 1935.

9. G. F. Gause, O. K. Nastukova, and W. W. Alpatov, The influence of biologically conditioned media on the growth of a mixed population of *Paramecium caudatum* and *P. aurelia*, *J. Anim. Ecol.*, *3*:222–30, 1934; G. F. Gause and A. A. Witt, Behavior of mixed populations and the problem of natural selection, *Amer. Nat.*, *69*:596–609, 1935.

10. T. Park, E. V. Gregg, and C. Z. Lutherman, Studies in population physiology: *X*, Interspecific competition in populations of granary beetles, *Physiol. Zool.*, *14*:395–430, 1941.

11. T. Park, Experimental studies of interspecific competition: *I*, Comparison between populations of the fluor beetles, *Tribolium confusum* Duval and *T. castaneum* Herbst, *Ecol. Monogr.*, *18*:205–308, 1948.

12. A. C. Crombie, On intraspecific and interspecific competition in larvae of graminivorous insects, *J. Exp. Biol.*, *20*:135–51, 1944; Further experiments in insect competition, *Proc. R. Soc. London* (B), *133*:76–109, 1946; Interspecific competition, *J. Anim. Ecol.*, *16*:44–73, 1947.

13. P. W. Frank, A laboratory study of intraspecies and interspecies competition in *Daphnia pulicaria* (Forbes) and *Simocephalus vetulus* O. F. Muller, *Physiol. Zool.*, *25*:178–204, 1952; Coactions in laboratory populations of two species of *Daphnia*, *Ecology*, *38*:510–19, 1957.

stance, states that after a sufficiently long time, if competition is occurring under certain conditions, the population of one species will tend to zero. It is some such qualitative prediction that the experimenter sets out to confirm.

In building the mathematical model and in its confirmation there are certain obvious postulates that underlie the theory and the procedure of confirmation. Since if the model is logically adequate, and yet is not confirmed, something must be wrong with the postulates, and since this may be of great scientific interest, it is worthwhile to inquire into the nature of these postulates in the present case. They appear to be:

1. The ordinary axioms of classical mathematical analysis. These are usually accepted; if anyone has a feeling that populations do not exhibit continuity or has Berkeleian objections to infinitesimals, he can always devote his spare time to restatements in finite difference form. Such statements are of course terribly clumsy.

2. A set of postulates which ultimately involve the large-scale conservation laws for matter and energy, and also a generally acceptable description of single-species populations reproducing under conditions of limited resources. The exact form of this description may be the subject of debate, but for any monotonic deterministic growth curve of a biologically possible kind, the qualitative outcome will be the same;[14] stochastic theory also exists[15] which gives the same ultimate

14. C. P. Winsor, Mathematical analysis of the growth of mixed populations, *Cold Spring Harbor Symp. Quant. Biol.*, 2:181–87, 1934.

15. W. Feller, Die Grundlagen von Volterraschen Theorie des Kampfes ums Dasein in wahrscheinlichkeitstheoretischer Behandlung, *Acta Biotheoret.*, 5:11–40, 1939; J. Neyman, T. Park, and E. L. Scott, Struggle for existence: The *Tribolium* model, biological and statistical aspects, *Proc. 3d Berkeley Symposium on Mathematical Statistics and Probability*, 4:41–79, 1959; M. S. Bartlett, On theoretical models for competitive and predatory biological systems, *Biometrika*, 44:27–42, 1957; P. H. Leslie and J. C. Grover, The properties of a stochastic model for two competing species, *Biometrika*, 45:316–30, 1958.

result except the nature of the surviving species may be determined probabilistically. Analogue computer studies show the same sort of result under conditions in which initially oscillations may occur.[16]

3. A set of rules about how experiments are to be accomplished. The experimenter obviously may not confirm the principle of competitive exclusion by arbitrarily removing all individuals of one of two species competing for the same niche during the early phases of the experiment. The rules are essentially practical interpretations of the theory; since the theory says at equilibrium, a rule is implied that the experiment goes on long enough to give confidence that equilibrium is reached.

4. A special postulate appearing in the theory, stated by Hardin as the Axiom of Inequality, may be isolated from 2. The axiom in essence states that no two natural bodies or collections of such bodies of more than subatomic or perhaps somewhat greater size are ever identical in their properties. The qualification about size is introduced as the axiom would apparently be false if applied to electrons.[17] It may be accepted as a quasi-empirical postulate based on the fact that all the objects to which it applies are likely to be composed of an indefinite number of parts in various states. At least in dealing with organisms and populations the possibility of quite identical properties is obviously exceedingly small. A more rigorous statement could no doubt be given. It is however important to note that apart from implying differences, the axiom does not say how great or how significant these may be. We have under 3 noted the rule about attainment of equilibrium. In the present case this is clearly related to the axiom of inequality. If at equilibrium a difference, namely survival or extinction, appears resulting from differences in properties of two populations, the smaller the latter difference, the longer we should expect to

16. P. J. Wangersky and W. J. Cunningham, Time lags in population models, *Cold Spring Harbor Symp. Quant. Biol.*, 22:329–38, 1957.
17. W. H. McCrea, Why are all electrons alike? *Nature*, 202:537–38, 1964.

have to wait for the former difference to appear. The axiom merely suggests that if we wait long enough it will.

It should be, but probably is not, unnecessary to add that if we are talking about competition and competitive exclusion, we must be sure that competition is actually involved and not commensalism or symbiosis. In the mathematical treatment of competition, if certain quantities appear as positive, there will be an equivalent theory of symbiosis if they are negative and of commensalism in certain cases if some are negative and some positive.

The differential equations based on logistic growth of populations (N_1, N_2) of single species (S_1, S_2) with linear competition functions are well known as:

$$\frac{dN_1}{dt} = b_1 N_1 \left(\frac{K_1 - N_1 - \alpha N_2}{K_1} \right)$$

$$\frac{dN_2}{dt} = b_2 N_2 \left(\frac{K_2 - N_2 - \beta N_1}{K_2} \right)$$

which, if the competition coefficients are positive quantities α and β, give qualitative results at equilibrium of the kind set out in the accompanying tabulation.

Relative Magnitude of Competition Coefficients	Results
$\alpha > K_1/K_2, \beta > K_2/K_1$	species initially commonest survives
$\alpha < K_1/K_2, \beta > K_2/K_1$	only S_1 survives
$\alpha > K_1/K_2, \beta < K_2/K_1$	only S_2 survives
$\alpha < K_1/K_2, \beta < K_2/K_1$	both S_1 and S_2 survive

The last case corresponds to the condition that each individual of both species *inhibits the growth of the conspecific population more than of the other population*. This is all that is required for coexistence. The condition can be realized geometrically by part of the habitat of each species being inaccessible to the other, so constituting a refuge from the effects of the other species. Both in experiments, notably those of Gause in which *Paramecium bursaria* was used, and in nature, such refuges may develop, but since we often find species that are clearly in different niches, moving around in the same space, a purely intensive definition of the niche, but one that retains its geometrical character, is desirable.

Formal nature of the niche

The intensive definition required may be obtained by considering a hyperspace, every coordinate $(X_1, X_2, X_3 \ldots)$ of which corresponds to a relevant variable in the life of a species of organism. A hypervolume can therefore be constructed, every point of which corresponds to a set of values of the variables permitting the organism to exist. If no competitors are present the hypervolume will constitute the *fundamental niche*[18] of the species. If a number of species are living together but competing, each will have a *realized niche* usually corresponding to a smaller hypervolume than the fundamental niche, but by the principle of competitive exclusion, no point in one realized niche is also in another. This presentation allows for the fact that the direction of competition can change with changing environmental conditions.[19] In constructing the hyperspace the coordinates can be graduated in any convenient way. If some represent *different proportions* of kinds of food

18. G. E. Hutchinson, Concluding remarks, *Cold Spring Harbor Symp. Quant. Biol.*, 22:415–27, 1958.
19. The first clear cases published were perhaps those of the stream planarians studied by R. S. A. Beauchamp and P. Ullyott, Competitive relationships between certain species of freshwater triclads, *J. Ecol.*, 20:200–08, 1932. The phenomenon is well known in laboratory experiments with both protozoa and grain and flour insects; see Gause, Nastukova, and Alpatov (above, n. 9); Park (above, n. 11); Crombie (above, n. 12).

it is possible for instance to get clean separations of the niches of species differing mainly in the proportions of food eaten, as in the titmice *(Parus)* studied by Betts.[20] The abstract niche is in fact constructed in order to be that thing in which two sympatric species do not live. This may sound artificial, but it does permit us to gain a great deal of insight during the process of designing niches in our minds for any species in which we are interested.

Examples of niche diversification

The number of really well-analyzed cases of closely allied species living together is still small, though not so small that they can all be conveniently considered. The examples to be given here, and in some of the later paragraphs involving special problems, are chosen primarily to illustrate the rather considerable variety of patterns that may be observed.

Although they are usually put in separate genera by mammalogists, the two African species of rhinoceros (Fig. 1) are of particular interest as the largest species of terrestrial animal that are essentially sympatric in part of their range today. In Zululand the two species still live close enough together,[21] though in somewhat different habitats, for their paths potentially to cross, and this was probably true in the past in many areas at the periphery of the former ranges of the white rhinoceros. The differences in distribution of the two species, where they occur in the same general region, are due in part to different habitat requirements and so to niche specificity. The square-lipped or white rhinoceros, *Ceratotherium simum,* is a grazing species living in open grassland; the black rhinoceros, *Diceros bicornis,* with pointed prehensile lips, the upper lip

20. M. M. Betts, The food of titmice in oak woodland, *J. Anim. Ecol.,* 24:282–323, 1955.

21. R. I. G. Atwell, Last strongholds of rhinoceros, *African Wildlife,* 2:35–52, 1948.

Fig. 1. The two species of rhinoceros living in Africa: *above* the white, square-lipped, or Burchell's rhinoceros, *Ceratotherium simum; below* the black or hook-lipped rhinoceros, *Diceros bicornis.* (Original from available sources, including living specimens in the Bronx Zoological Gardens, by W. Vars.)

having a hook-like profile, mainly browses on bushes and so does not inhabit areas devoid of such taller vegetation. Along with this main ecological difference, correlated with the structure of the animals, there are various behavioral differences which can partly, but by no means entirely, be correlated with the primary difference in the mode of life. *Ceratotherium simum*, which keeps moving as it grazes, is less stationary than *D. bicornis*, though unlike the latter it builds dunghills which probably have territorial significance. It is moreover more likely to occur in small parties, perhaps of family origin, than is the more aggressive *D. bicornis*, which lives either solitarily or in pairs. It is said that the calf of the latter usually follows its mother while that of *C. simum* habitually runs ahead of the cow, though this behavior difference seems to break down if the animals are frightened.

Since the species are often placed in different genera and probably have a fairly long history of phyletic separation, it is not surprising to find a good deal of divergence, not only in food habits and concomitant structure, which affect teeth as well as lips, but also in behavior relating to a number of types of activity other than nutrition.

Another mammalian case in which actual competition evidently can occur in nature has been beautifully analyzed by Miller.[22] This case involves four species of pocket gopher in Colorado. The optimal conditions for all species are provided by deep light soils, but when in competition they can be arranged in a series *Geomys bursarius, Cratogeomys castanops, Thomomys bottae,* and *T. talpoides,* the first tending to displace all other species and the last none, in favorable habitats. The sizes of the fundamental niches, however, are related inversely to the competitive ability in an optimal habitat, so that *G. bursarius* lives in the best terrain because it can displace all species there but cannot invade the less suitable ground, while *T. tal-*

22. R. S. Miller, Ecology and distribution of pocket gophers (Geomyidae) in Colorado, *Ecology, 45:*256–72, 1964.

poides, though it potentially has the largest fundamental niche, usually exists in marginally poor habitats unsuitable for the other species. This case in fact provides an example of the reciprocal relationship between adaptability (or large fundamental niche) and adaptation (or possessing inherent competitive powers) that has been stressed by Gause[23] in another context.

The next three cases relate to birds; they do not exhaust the possible kinds of niche diversification in the group, but they are very instructive.

White[24] has described the case of three species of *Ploceus* nesting along the shores of Lake Mweru in Central Africa and feeding in bush not far from the lake margin. The three species are very similar in appearance but *Ploceus intermedius cabanisii* was feeding exclusively on small black seeds, *P. melanocephalus duboisii* on green seeds probably of grasses, while *P. cucullatus nigriceps* was eating insects. *P. melanocephalus duboisii* and *P. cucullatus nigriceps* were mixed up together in their colonial nests. It is just possible that their difference in food primarily implies a difference in breeding time; the birds catching insects may have been rearing young. Though there is clear niche separation implied by White's observations, it is by no means certain that it would be maintained in the same manner throughout the year.

A case in some ways the reciprocal of that just described is provided by the vesper sparrow, *Pooecetes gramineus,* the field sparrow, *Spizella pusilla,* and the chipping sparrow, *S. passerina,* studied by Evans[25] in Michigan. Here the rather mixed diet differed little between the species but they show differences in

23. G. F. Gause, Problems of evolution, *Trans. Conn. Acad. Arts Sci.,* 37:17–68, 1947.

24. C. M. N. White, Weaver birds at Lake Mweru, *Ibis, 93:*626–27, 1951.

25. F. C. Evans, The food of vesper, field and chipping sparrows nesting in an abandoned field in southeastern Michigan, *Amer. Midl. Nat.,* 72:57–75, 1964.

nesting site, *P. gramineus* being an exclusively ground-nesting species, *S. passerina* exclusively using bushes and trees, and *S. pusilla* behaving in an intermediate way. It is possible that some preferences for particular strata are involved throughout the whole ecology of the birds.

A case in which very definite behavioral responses to habitat permit a number of congeneric species of comparable size and structure to live together is provided by MacArthur's[26] admirable study of five members of the genus *Dendroica* in the spruce forests of Maine (Fig. 2). Not only does each species tend to live and feed in a particular zone in and below the spruce tree, but behavioral differences must further cause specific differences in the probability of a given insect on the tree being eaten by any species of warbler. In essence the five species differ in the following way.

Dendroica tigrina, Cape May warbler: feeds in the peripheral zone of the upper part of the tree, modal nesting height 12 m., mean interval between flights 8.6 seconds, movement in tree predominantly vertical, long flights from tree to tree common, may feed in low vegetation in bad weather, hawks for flying insects but also spends much time eating sedentary prey, breeds early.

D. coronata, myrtle warbler: feeds mainly but by no means exclusively in lower parts of tree and between branches and ground, modal nesting height 4–5 m., mean interval between flights 7.5 seconds, movement in tree tangential, vertical, and radial, the former two predominating slightly over the third, long flights common, may hunt by hawking insects on wing or by rapid peering for sedentary prey, breeds early.

D. virens, black-throated green warbler: mainly feeds in the peripheral and intermediate zones of the middle of the tree, modal nesting height 4.5 m., mean interval between flights 5.5 seconds, movement in tree predominantly tangential, the

26. R. H. MacArthur, Population ecology of some warblers of northeastern coniferous forests, *Ecology, 39*:599–619, 1958.

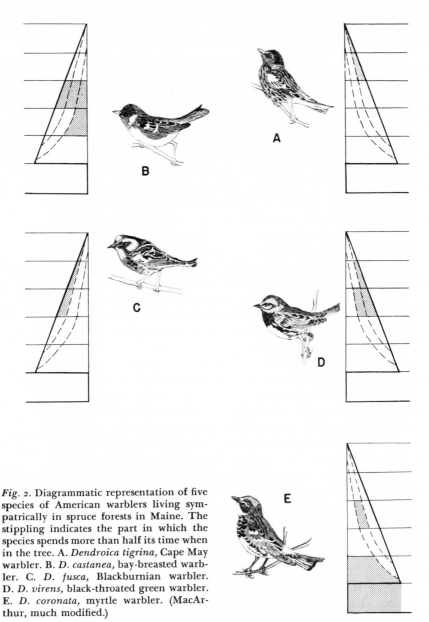

Fig. 2. Diagrammatic representation of five species of American warblers living sympatrically in spruce forests in Maine. The stippling indicates the part in which the species spends more than half its time when in the tree. A. *Dendroica tigrina,* Cape May warbler. B. *D. castanea,* bay-breasted warbler. C. *D. fusca,* Blackburnian warbler. D. *D. virens,* black-throated green warbler. E. *D. coronata,* myrtle warbler. (MacArthur, much modified.)

bird appearing the most nervous of the five, long flights rare, hovers taking sedentary or slowly moving food among foliage from below, rarely hawks for flying food and then inefficiently, prolonged intermediate breeding season.

D. fusca, Blackburnian warbler: mainly feeds in the peripheral zone in the upper part of the tree, modal nesting height 15 m., mean interval between flights 7.5 seconds, movement in tree predominantly radial, long flights very rare, the apical parts of branches being systematically explored for food, very little hawking of flying insects, breeding season as in *D. virens.*

D. castanea, bay-breasted warbler: mainly feeds in the lower and middle parts of the tree, partly in the central as well as the intermediate and peripheral zones, modal nesting height 3 m., mean interval between flights 12.5 seconds, much the most placid species, main movement radial, feeding like the preceding but lower, some long flights observed, both hawking and hovering observed, latest breeder of the five.

It is evident that both the regions in which food is sought and the mode of seeking it will insure very considerable differences in diet, which have indeed been observed. Even more, the probability of different specimens of the same fairly eurytopic insect falling prey when in different parts of the tree must differ greatly from species to species. Practically all the differences which separate the niches of these birds are behavioral, though the Cape May warbler has a more tubular tongue and is able to feed from flowers in poor weather.

The myrtle warbler appears to have the widest fundamental niche, but maintains a low constant population, perhaps being limited somewhat by competition with more adapted but less adaptable species. In general its behavior in the spruce forest is similar to that of the Cape May save the myrtle tends to live lower and the Cape May higher in the trees. The species differ biologically in that the Cape May warbler is an opportunistic and somewhat fugitive species, dependent largely on outbreaks of spruce budworm.

The Blackburnian and bay-breasted constitute a pair moving radially in their search for food, but again differing in the altitude explored—the Blackburnian is the species of the upper, the bay-breasted of the lower, parts of the tree. Here the bay-breasted is the opportunistic fugitive species, able to adjust its clutch size to food abundance, which the Blackburnian, black-throated green, and myrtle warblers seem unable to do.

The black-throated green differs from the other species in its tangential movement and hovering mode of feeding.

Turning to the larger invertebrates, one of the most impressive cases is provided by the cone shells of the genus *Conus*, studied by Kohn.[27] The genus consists of many hundreds of living species, which have received about 2,600 names. They are most abundant in the Indo-Pacific region, in some parts of which over fifty species may occur in littoral and moderately deep water off a given coastline. The species are all very closely allied structurally and the validity of most of the subgenera that have been proposed to order the vast number of species is questionable.

In Figure 3, the distribution of the six species normally found on wave-cut benches around Hawaii is indicated from Kohn's work on the coast of Kauai, off Oahu. The main biological characteristics of the species, proceeding in their order of commonness from the landward to the seaward margin of the bench and so roughly in order of decreasing exposure to air at low tide, are as follows:

C. sponsalis, the smallest species, nearly always on algal turf, binding sand, feeds both on Nereidae and Eunicidae, the only species to eat the small *Nereis* cf. *jacksoni.*

C. abbreviatus, mainly on algal turf but more often on bare

27. A. J. Kohn, The ecology of *Conus* in Hawaii, *Ecol. Monogr.*, 29:47–90, 1959. For an estimate of the number of specific names see A. J. Kohn, Type specimens and identity of the described species of *Conus: I,* The species described by Linnaeus 1758–1767, *J. Linn. Soc. London Zool., 44*:740–68, 1963.

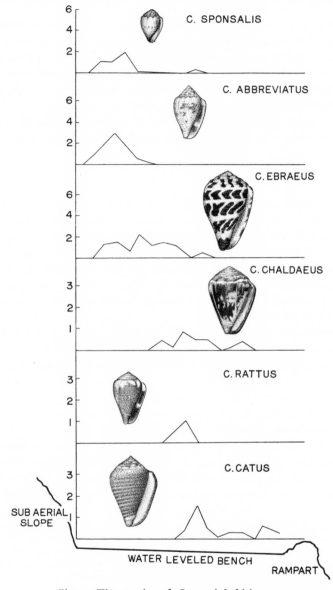

Fig. 3. The species of *Conus* inhabiting a wave-cut littoral bench in Hawaii, with the distribution of individuals along a transect from the landward to the seaward edge. (Modified from Kohn, with original drawings by W. Vars.)

sand or rock than the preceding, feeds mainly on Eunicidae, though *Perinereis helleri* may be taken in fair numbers.

C. ebraeus, mainly on algal turf, but a third of occurrences on bare sand or rock, feeds almost exclusively on *P. helleri.*

C. chaldaeus, mainly on bare sand or rock, feeds almost entirely on *Platynereis dumerilii.*

C. rattus, predominantly on algal turf but a quarter of the occurrences on bare rock, feeds mainly on *Eunice antennata* and *P. helleri.*

C. catus, mainly on bare rock and sand, feeds exclusively on fish.

In other habitats in slightly deeper water, other species able to bring down fish with their long poisonous radula teeth occur; there is also a species feeding largely on enteropneusts, and others entirely on mollusks, in one case primarily on other species of *Conus.* It is evident that in ability to tolerate varying degrees of exposure to air at low tide, in substrate preference, and in feeding habits and food preferences this assemblage of species, some found with the same habits from Hawaii to the Seychelles, has developed extreme niche specificity permitting an extraordinary number of sympatric species to co-occur.

While behavior is probably more important than structural adaptation in the genus, part of the difference in food may involve size differences and small differences in the radula tooth, which in some cases is apparently adapted to tearing off the tubes of eunicid worms.

In many groups of animals the behavioral differences are much less, and structural differences, at their simplest a mere difference in size, are of primary importance. Very good examples are probably to be found in the copepods of lakes and ponds, where size differences, as Fryer[28] has found, are clearly related to differences in food. It is interesting that in the rather

28. G. Fryer, Contributions to our knowledge of the biology and systematics of the freshwater Copepoda, *Schw. Zeitsch. Hydrol.,* 16:64–77, 1954.

difficult habitats provided by temporary waters, such as those of semiarid regions, the size differences in co-occurring diaptomid copepods are apt to be accentuated, as in the characteristic pair of very closely allied if generically separated members of the Paradiaptominae from the large, temporary dilute pans of the Transvaal, namely *Lovenula falcifera* and *Metadiaptomus transvaalensis* (Fig. 4).

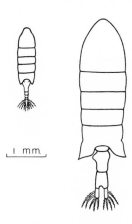

Fig. 4. The small diaptomid copepod *Metadiaptomus transvaalensis* and its large relative *Lovenula falcifera*, living together in the less mineralized and temporary pans of the Transvaal. (Original, in part modified from G. O. Sars.)

One of the most perfect cases of niche diversification within a single genus comes from Bērziņš'[29] study of the rotifers of Skärshultsjön, a small lake in central Sweden (Fig. 5). Here at the height of summer, among species of other genera, five members of the genus *Polyarthra* coexist. In the epilimnion there are three species, namely *P. euryptera*, ordinarily 160 to

29. B. Bērziņš, Ein planktologisches Querprofil, *Inst. Freshwater Res. Drottningholm*, rep. no. 39 (1958), pp. 5–22.

210 μ long, *P. vulgaris,* ordinarily 100 to 145 μ long, and *P. remata,* ordinarily 80 to 120 μ long, the last and smallest being somewhat more littoral than the other two. In the moderately cool but well-oxygenated waters of the metalimnion, *P. major* is found, while *P. longiremis* occurs in summer only in the deep, cold, and partly deoxygenated waters of the hypolimnion. These animals feed mainly on flagellates, being particularly partial

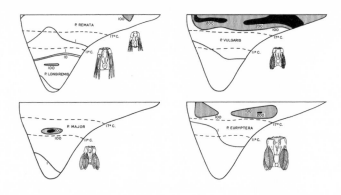

Fig. 5. Distribution of the species of *Polyarthra* in a section across Skärshultsjön in Sweden, with diagrammatic sketches (x 40) of the five animals involved. (Modified from the diagrams of Bērziņš with sketches derived from all available sources.)

to cryptomonads. It is reasonable, as in other cases, to suppose that the large, medium, and small species tend to feed on large, medium, and small food, while the depth distribution probably reflects the temperature and oxygen concentration tolerances and preferrenda. It is easy to see that if proportion of food of various sizes, temperature, and oxygen concentration were the three variables under consideration, the niches of all five species here considered as plotted with three coordinates could be nonoverlapping, even though the habitats of two of the epilimnetic species were completely identical and that of the third almost so. The case is particularly instructive, even though only partially analyzed, because it shows, in a single small body of water in which the paths of any species might, on purely mechanical grounds, intersect, three species that must in fact cross each other's paths all the time and two more that do so less often if at all. In the first case the niche separation is presumably largely based on size differences, while in the second behavioral differences ensuring spatial separation in the lake are obviously involved.

Apparent exceptions to competitive exclusion

In view of the fact that a good many cases will occur to most naturalists who have a wide and deep knowledge of a given flora or fauna, that look very odd from the standpoint of competitive exclusion, it is desirable to examine the kinds of apparent exception that may occur.

A most convincing type of seeming exception, in which apparently complete niche identity is possible in co-occurring species, could develop in territorial species in which all competition for territory is intraspecific. It was the possibility of this happening that first directed MacArthur to the problem of the niches of warblers in a coniferous forest, but in this case a very clear set of separate niches was elucidated. A case however has turned up in Marshall's[30] admirable study of the brown towhee, *Pipilo fuscus mesoleucus,* and the Abert towhee, *P. aberti,* which seems from the available information to provide a case of what we had been looking for (Fig. 6). The principle involved is that if the equilibrium populations are set solely by the areas available for territory, food and all other resources being in excess for the combined equilibrium populations for both

30. J. T. Marshall, Interrelations of Abert and brown towhees, *Condor,* 62:49–64, 1960.

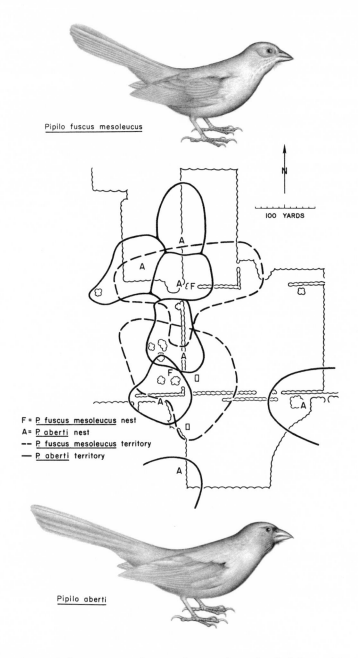

Fig. 6. *Pipilo fuscus mesoleucus* (*above*) and *P. aberti* (*below*) with maps of overlapping territory to illustrate Marshall's work.

species, then provided the competition for territories is solely intraspecific, each species behaving as if the other were not there, coexistence is possible. In terms of the formal model of the niche, each species has an axis corresponding to potential territory density graduated from zero to maximum possible density, but it is defined solely in terms of its own territory. In the niche hyperspace there is thus an axis with a positive range of values for one species and zero for the other, and another axis with zero value for the first and a positive range for the second. This gives complete formal niche separation. The example is therefore not an exception, but a very interesting special case, of the principle of competitive exclusion.

A second apparent type of exception, realized in the laboratory by Slobodkin[31] in his experiments with *Hydra,* depends on the possibility that a difference of susceptibility to predation can be the basis of niche diversification. We suppose that we have two species, one rather more efficient than the other so that in competition the first species would displace the second. We now introduce a predator which feeds selectively on the first species. If the intensity of predation is properly adjusted to the vital statistical properties of the two species and the competition coefficients when they co-occur, a mixed population is possible. Unfortunately really good unequivocal examples from nature do not yet seem available.

A third type of exception is that discussed independently, and almost simultaneously, by Skellam[32] and myself, involving what I then termed fugitive species. The principle is that if one species is more mobile than another, and if suitable local environments are always being formed, then even though the

31. L. B. Slobodkin, *Growth and Regulation of Animal Populations,* New York, 1961. J. L. Brooks and S. I. Dodson now appear to be finding this phenomenon of great importance in the zooplankton.

32. J. G. Skellam, Random dispersal in theoretical populations, *Biometrika, 38:*196–218, 1951; G. E. Hutchinson, Copepodology for the ornithologist, *Ecology, 32:*571–77, 1951.

mobile or fugitive species is ultimately always locally displaced by a competitor, it can survive by always being in the process of establishing itself on a new site which the competitor has not yet reached. Skellam developed the idea formally for two species of annual plants. Here the deaths of the previous generation in the autumn clear sites for the new generation. In this case the fugitive species appears to be living in the same community as its competitor because the size of the site required is not large, in fact may be small relative to that of the observer. Such cases would then appear to be exceptions to the competitive exclusion principle. I developed the idea, derived ultimately from Elton, for freshwater copepods invading newly built dams and other artificial waters. Here the habitats are large relative to the observer and still larger relative to the animals involved. In such cases the fugitive species might build up a large population, which then would succumb to competition, but we should not regard the phenomenon as an example of an exception to competitive exclusion, indeed just the reverse. Here our point of view, as is often the case in ecology, depends on the scale and grain-size of the environment.

A very interesting fourth type of exception is provided by Ross'[33] work on the six species of the leafhopper *Erythroneura* of the *lawsoni*-group living on sycamores (*Platanus occidentalis*) in Illinois. Up to five species may occur on a single tree. There are evidently slight differences in tolerance among the species, *E. lawsoni* being the only consistent inhabitant of trees in open, wind-swept, dry situations, while *E. morgani* and *E. bella* almost always occur in humid valleys. Evidence of interspecific competition is meager and it is suggested that, in general, density-independent factors tend to limit the sizes of populations, but that there are enough slight differences in tolerance to insure that locally one species may be dominant, as is usually observed;

33. H. H. Ross, Principles of natural coexistence indicated by leafhopper populations, *Evolution, 11*:113–29, 1957.

from such foci the various species easily invade neighboring habitats where mixed populations build up. The situation in fact is comparable to the fugitive species of the previous paragraphs except that all species are fugitive, and in essence involves the coexistence, in any region, of localities specially favorable for each species, high vagility, and failure to attain equilibrium in most habitats. It is quite probable that this type of situation is a usual one in rapidly reproducing mobile phytophagous insects; it seems likely to be particularly common in the auchenorrhynchous Homoptera where genera containing enormous numbers of species have developed. Much further work on what actually happens in natural and experimental populations of these fascinating insects is clearly needed.

It is quite possible[34] that a somewhat similar phenomenon may underlie the paradoxical situation presented by the multispecific associations of autotrophic phytoplankton in the freely circulating upper waters of lakes and the ocean in which most species must be competing for the very limited supply of a relatively small number of mineral nutrients in an environment that does not provide much possibility of geometrical fractionation corresponding to niche specificity. This case or group of cases provides quite as conspicuous an example of an apparent exception to the principle as do the leafhoppers, and it is tempting to look for an explanation of a formally equivalent sort. In some cases the competition may only be apparent and the association conceivably could be determined by commensal or symbiotic relationships. Thus if the potentially more efficient competitor were dependent on the less efficient competitor for a vitamin secreted into the water, under some conditions a stable association would be possible. The possibility of niche diversification of a special sort by predation has already been mentioned. It may well occur in the phytoplankton on which many rotifers

34. G. E. Hutchinson, The paradox of the plankton, *Amer. Nat.*, 95:137–45, 1961.

and crustaceans prey considerably more selectively than was once thought likely.[35] In an earlier paper [36] it was suggested that in many cases in the phytoplankton, no equilibrium is achieved before conditions of light, temperature, chemistry, or predation change sufficiently for one potential dominant to be superseded by another, which however never gets a chance to exclude its competitors before another change takes place. This suggestion is in accord with the rather irregular but nevertheless seasonal changes that are observed. It has the disadvantage[37] of implying a good deal of random extinction, as changing conditions become for short times very unfavorable to species that happened to be rather rare. The general persistence of species over fairly long periods of time, frequently observed in lake-sediment studies, therefore appears to militate against the explanation in its simplest form. Since any species that has occurred in a locality can live there in some circumstances, there is an appreciable chance of reestablishment, at least temporarily, if it can be reintroduced. This is in fact the *Erythroneura* situation. Where many interconnected small lakes, or very large lakes containing partially discrete water masses, are involved, this may be possible. Where resting stages are produced they may easily permit a species to tide over periods of extinction of the active form[38] though unfortunately at least in the desmids, planktonic life seems to inhibit their produc-

35. For rotifers see particularly summaries given by B. Pejler, Taxonomical and ecological studies on planktonic Rotatoria from northern Swedish Lapland, *K. Svenska Vetensk.Akad. Handl.* Fjärde ser. bd. 6, no. 5, 68 pp.; and W. T. Edmondson, Reproductive rate of planktonic rotifers as related to food and temperature in nature (*in press*); for copepods see Fryer (above, n. 28).

36. G. E. Hutchinson, Ecological aspects of succession in natural populations, *Amer. Nat.*, 75:406–18, 1941. See also above, n. 34.

37. R. H. MacArthur, verbal communication. Cf. L. C. Cole, Competitive exclusion, *Science, 132*:348–49, 1960.

38. G. E. Hutchinson, The lacustrine microcosm reconsidered, *Amer. Sci.*, 52:334–41, 1964 (reprinted in this volume).

tion.[39] It is also possible[40] that many populations of planktonic species are merely enormous opportunistic expansions of benthic populations, the planktonic individuals playing little part in permanently carrying on the species, while the persistent benthic specimens in quite discrete niches do this and so play the part of resting stages.

It must also be realized that in a lake, say 10 meters deep and one square kilometer in area, a species with a total population of 10^7 individuals would appear so rare to the planktologist that he would never find it. MacArthur[41] notes that the final phases of extinction may proceed very slowly in realistic models so that the principle of competitive exclusion may in practice really amount to a proposition that one of two species must be very rare if it is habitually found living in the same niche as a competitor. This weak form of the principle may well apply to unicellular planktonic organisms when very rare means less than 10^7 in a continuous habitat!

In the open ocean reintroduction from the littoral benthos or other refugium is essentially impossible. It has already been indicated that although the theory depends on an axiom of inequality, there is no a priori criterion as to how unequal the two species must be nor, as we have just emphasized, how slowly competitive exclusion may occur. Riley[42] suggests that autotrophic phytoplanktonic organisms may approach so closely some asymptotic level of possible adaptation, with such small differences between them, that when they compete the replacement of one by another proceeds so slowly that it is unobservable.

39. J. W. G. Lund, Edgardo Baldi Memorial Lecture, Primary productivity and periodicity of phytoplankton, *Verh. int. Ver. Limnol.*, 15:37–56, 1964.

40. The idea is due to Dr. Ruth Patrick; see also above, n. 34.

41. Personal communication.

42. G. A. Riley, *Marine Biology I*, 1st Internat. Interdisciplinary Conference, AIBS, Washington, 1963; see pp. 69–70.

In considering all these exceptions it would seem that in most cases we have a plethora of potential explanations. It appears likely that, though in no case do we fully understand what is happening, no grand principle invalidating the general applicability of competitive exclusion, when it is applicable, has been overlooked. Rather it seems that each apparent exception would fall into place in a general theory including all the special kinds of phenomena that have been discussed, even though we do not yet have enough knowledge to choose which particular explanation fits a particular case.

The niche in allopatric speciation

Before proceeding to examine several possible kinds of niche diversification it is worthwhile to look at the current concepts of evolution at the species level to see how well they fit in with the point of view here being developed.

The type of speciation, at least in animals, that we have come to regard as typical[43] involves some separation of initially continuous populations, a period of evolutionary speciation in two slightly different habitats and reinvasion of one species range by the other, or of course mutual reinvasion. This process almost inevitably involves niche separation; the two species have had different histories and so will differ a little in their adaptation. If they can coexist by virtue of these differences

43. The importance of initial geographic isolation was first made clear by Moritz Wagner (*Die Darwin'sche Theorie und das Migrationsgesetz der Organismen,* Leipzig, 1868); most of the subsequent proponents of the idea were taxonomists and field naturalists whose work was largely dismissed by experimental biologists and geneticists. During the present century some of the best systematists, notably Karl Jordan, championed the idea effectively, and in recent years it has become almost universally recognized as correct, largely due to the work of Ernst Mayr, whose most recent book, *Animal Species and Evolution* (Cambridge, Mass., 1963), contains in chap. 16 an admirable history of the development of ideas about allopatric speciation. Reading this chapter, in which it becomes clear how many progressive modern biologists were wrong and how certain supposedly conservative museum men were right, should be very salutary.

they will, unless they have become very different, both compete for parts of the same original fundamental niche and survival in the two realized niches will be increased, and competition lessened, by any specializations enabling the new niches to be better utilized with a minimum of attempted transgression. The classical evolutionary play thus practically involves the continual diversification of the biota as long as conditions remain reasonably but not completely stable and small but not great changes in stage set occur. It is reasonable to suppose that if the process could continue indefinitely an asymptotic approach to a certain maximum in number of niches and so of species would result. Some investigators have believed that in stable tropical areas the maximum is indeed approached by certain groups. There is however much need for investigation on the problem as to how far the division of niche space is possible.

Although this type of evolution is now usually regarded as almost self-evident, the number of cases in which it is clearly occurring is still not very great. As most described cases are from vertebrates or butterflies, I illustrate one by way of variety from the notonectid water bugs of the genus *Anisops* (Fig. 7). Here we have a group of species[44] in which the two claws of the middle legs are quite different in shape in the male. Since in the female and in all other species of the family, as indeed in nearly all Hemiptera, the intermediate claws are alike, we may regard this group of species as specialized. Within the group there is clearly a tendency for the males to have a protuberance between the eyes in front of the head, and in some species this is quite large. Three particularly closely allied species, *A. sardea,* *A. bouvieri,* and *A. extendofrons,* are probably the most specialized species of the genus and have very produced heads in the males. It is hard to arrange the other seventy-odd species in species groups or subgenera, and I assume that many are quite old descendants of numerous independent lines. In Central

44. G. T. Brooks, A revision of the genus *Anisops* (Notonectidae, Hemiptera), *Univ. Kansas Sci. Bull.,* 34:304–519, 1951.

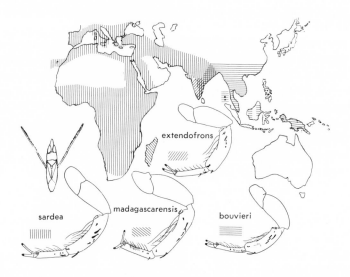

Fig. 7. Distribution of four very closely allied species of *Anisops,* showing a relatively small area in eastern India where three species are sympatric, with a sketch of *A. sardea* ♂ (x 1.6), and of the main diagnostic features of the anterior leg of the ♂ of all four species. (Original, in part after Brooks.) The range of *A. bouvieri* between the mainland of southeast Asia and New Guinea is hypothetical; the species seems not to occur in Java and Sumatra. Apart from the published distribution, some manuscript records from collections made by the Yale North India Expedition are included in defining the areas occupied in India.

Africa there is often co-occurrence of apparently related small primitive species. The three most highly specialized species named above, however, appear to be partly allopatric and to be actually spreading; *A. sardea,* known from Spain to India and south through Africa, has not quite reached to the Cape Peninsula, though climatically it would be suitable and there are fewer competitors in South than in Central Africa. There is a very closely allied vicarious species or subspecies *madagascaren-*

sis in Madagascar, which may perhaps represent the primitive stock surviving in an insular refuge. The three longheaded forms all seem to be entering each other's ranges in India; at least in Eastern Central India they are sympatric. *Anisops* seems therefore to behave as twentieth-century exponents of evolutionary theory would have it behave. The fact that in so doing it has produced about ninety species, of which in many places up to ten may be sympatric and at least six may co-occur in small ponds, without any hint, except in some cases size differences which presumably imply differences in the size of food taken, as to what the specific differences mean, is merely a measure of our ignorance.

Specialization and spatial adaptation

The matter has been considered theoretically by MacArthur and Levins,[45] who conclude that two extreme types of niche specificity do in fact exist. In one the animal remains adaptable in its requirements but requires to be spatially separate from its closest allies and competitors, which usually involves special behavioral responses to the environment to keep the animal in the right place. In the other the various species are structurally specialized to use different resources; they do not need to have behavioral mechanisms fixing them in place and in fact cross each other's path. In a very large number of cases, a moderate difference in size, of the order of 130:100, provides sufficient difference to permit obligate feeding on different proportions of food. This is no doubt the simplest kind of structural difference.

When we have the possibility of a well-defined set of alterna-

45. R. MacArthur and R. Levins, Competition, habitat selection, and character displacement, *Proc. Nat. Acad. Sci., 51*:1207–10, 1964. See also R. Levins, Theory of fitness in a heterogeneous environment, *I: Amer. Nat., 96*:361–73, 1962; *II: Amer. Nat., 97*:75–90, 1963; *III: Jour. Theor. Biol., 7*:224–40, 1964.

tives as are given by an available deductive theory, it is probably useful to see how they work out in different groups. MacArthur and Levins give some examples from birds, and in general wherever we have raptorial species the size difference permitting some specialization and some degree of ecological sympatry is likely. Moreover the same situation seems to occur among filtering and sedimenting microphagous groups such as the calanoid copepods as well as the rotifers, as in the examples just given.

Among the large genera of plant bugs there is little evidence that such variation in size as occurs is involved in ecological separation, which must fundamentally be determined by behavior. Thus in the well-known fauna of Britain[46] there are seventeen species of the mirid genus *Orthotylus* (Fig. 8). Of these, eleven may be regarded as essentially monophagous, and even where there is a fair degree of polyphagy the plants preferred by the different polyphagous species tend not to be the same. Of the monophagous species three occur, in fact may co-occur, on broom, *Sarothamnus scoparius*. There is here more than a hint of niche separation. One species *O. virescens* has a shorter rostrum than the other two, which suggests a slightly different feeding site on the broom plant; of the two with longer rostra, *O. adenocarpi* tends to mature earlier than *O. concolor*.

Overall size seems to play no part in ecological separation. The largest species, *O. viridinervis,* 5 to 6 mm. long, is confined to witch elms (*Ulmus glabra*), while the two smallest, *O. rubidus* and *O. moncreaffii,* 2.7 to 3.3 mm. long, respectively, on *Salicornia* and on *Halimione* in salt marshes, are all more or less monophagous on plants not supporting competitors of the same genus.

This same picture would be given by a number of other genera, such as *Psallus* in the Miridae or *Anthocoris* in the Anthocoridae. It is interesting that the latter genus consists of predacious bugs, but several are confined to particular plants

46. T. R. E. Southwood and D. Leston, *Land and water bugs of the British Isles,* London and New York, 1959.

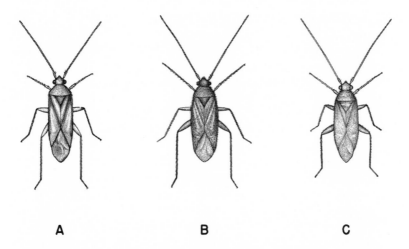

A   **B**   **C**

Fig. 8. Three species of *Orthotylus* found together on broom in Europe. A. *O. adenocarpi,* a yellowish or bluish-green species, appearing as an adult in late June. B. *O. virescens,* a deep green species, adult appearing in mid-July, rostrum shorter than in the other two. C. *O. concolor,* a pale green species, adults emerging late July. Apart from the differences in color and rostral length, the relative proportions of the segments of the antennae, the degree of hairiness, and the ♂ genitalia provide diagnostic characters, but the three species are clearly very closely allied (x 5). (Original drawings by W. Vars.)

on which they eat particular small phytophagous arthropods.[47] Thus *A. sarothamni* breeds only on broom feeding on the psyllids *Psylla spartiophila* and *Arytaina genistae* and to some extent on the aphid *Acyrthosiphon pisum. A. gallarum-ulmi* normally develops only on the gall-producing aphid *Eriosoma ulmi* on elm, though it occasionally occurs as an adult on other plants with aphid galls. *A. visci* lives on mistletoe, feeding on the psyllid *Psylla visci.* In these cases it is not unreasonable to

47. N. H. Anderson, Bionomics of the six species of *Anthocoris* (Heteroptera: Anthocoridae) in England, *Trans. R. Entom. Soc. London, 114:*67–95, 1962.

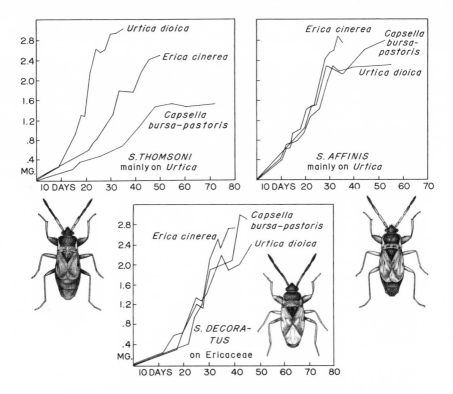

Fig. 9. Growth curves on various foods, from the experiments of Eyles, of the females of three common European species of *Scolopostethus*, which are illustrated (x 5). (Original drawings of W. Vars.)

suppose the bug initially seeks the plant rather than the insect prey, as if it were phytophagous.

A particularly interesting case is provided by Eyles'[48] recent study of the feeding of three very closely allied species of the lygaeid genus *Scolopostethus* (Fig. 9). These insects feed on seeds, and within the genus show some degree of habitat pref-

48. A. C. Eyles, Feeding habits of some Rhyparochrominae (Heteroptera: Lygaeidae) with particular reference to the value of natural foods, *Trans. R. Entom. Soc. London,* 116:89–114, 1964.

58

erence. *S. affinis* usually occurs on nettles, as does *S. thomsoni,* though perhaps it is a little more varied in its host plant than *S. affinis;* it probably normally occurs higher on the plant than does the latter. *S. decoratus* is found on *Erica* and *Calluna,* sometimes in vast numbers. What is known of the natural history of the three species suggests that position on the plant, perhaps associated with eating less mature seeds by *S. thomsoni,* as well as host plant specificity, would produce niche separation. It is therefore rather odd to find that *S. decoratus* as well as *S. affinis* grow equally well on *Urtica, Erica,* and *Capsella* seeds, though *S. thomsoni* does much better on *Urtica* than on *Erica* and much better on *Erica* than on *Capsella.* The mechanisms and meaning of habitat selection are clearly complicated and quite inadequately understood.

These examples serve to show how, with the evolution of suctorial mouth parts, adapted to feeding on plants or stationary insect plant-parasites, a great deal of specialization can be evolved behaviorally with a minimum of structural adaptation. The Homoptera, with its fantastic array of species of Cicadelloidea, doubtless would provide even more impressive examples. However, as soon as we pass to the hemipterous genera with species hunting more active prey, as in the Nabidae or Notonectidae, we begin to find just the same sort of size differences as in predacious mammals or birds, or in the microphagous rotifers and calanoid copepods. Thus in a single collection of *Anisops* from a pool 5 m. across in the bed of the Limpopo River near Messina, Transvaal, I noted[49] six species:

**A. sardea*	♂ 8.5–9.0 mm., ♀ 8.0–8.5 mm.
A. gracilis	7.0–8.0 mm.
A. varia scutellata	6.0–7.5 mm.
**A. debilis*	6.5–6.8 mm.
A. praetexta	5.5–6.5 mm.
**A. jaczewskii*	5.0–5.6 mm.

49. G. E. Hutchinson, A revision of the Notonectidae and Corixidae of South Africa, *Ann. S. Afr. Mus.,* 23:359–474, 1929.

The three species marked with asterisks—large, intermediate, and small, without overlap in size—were specifically noted as occurring together in the water in the shadow of a boulder around which the pool had been excavated in the sandy bed by the river in flood. It is probable that in Central Africa even more impressive assemblages occur; here the species can vary in size from 4.0 mm. in the male of *A. elegans* to 10.5 mm. in the female of *A. pellucens,* but there is almost nothing known about associations. The example from the Limpopo River does suggest that factors other than size are involved also; at the time the collections were made the taxonomy was in chaos and detailed field observations on the fine distribution therefore very difficult.

It is evident that the approach of MacArthur and Levins can be used to explore rather major kinds of difference in adaptation in large groups of organisms. Other comparable dichotomies also exist. Two, namely those involving the seasonal aspects and timing of the life histories and those involving polymorphism, will be explored. The mathematical reader should consult the works of Levins for such theoretical background as exists.

Types of temporal adaptation

Two very broad aspects of temporal adaptation may be considered.

Firstly we may consider the relationship of the length of life cycle to the probable period of relevant changes in the environment, distinguishing those species whose life history is short, of the same order of magnitude, or long, compared with such a period.[50] The environmental periods that are distinguishable are of differing lengths. Only three types are dependably periodic, namely the nocturno-diurnal or diel, lunar (in-

50. G. E. Hutchinson, The concept of pattern in ecology, *Proc. Acad. Nat. Sci. Phila., 105*:1–12, 1953.

cluding tidal), and annual cycles of celestial mechanical origin, the lunar cycle being less important than the other two. Between the nocturno-diurnal and lunar or annual cycles, irregular changes in weather with a period of a few days or a week or so are usual in temperate and some tropical regions.

Few, if any, populations could reach equilibrium, except in impoverished habitats not permitting growth or reproduction, in a fraction of a day. All populations in the illuminated parts of the biosphere, therefore, are subject to the daily light and temperature rhythms, but may be relatively uninfluenced by them, and by all longer variations while the populations persist. In some cases, however, equilibrium may be achieved well within the longer periods of environmental change, notably the annual cycle.

We may in fact generalize as follows. Considering any type of environmental fluctuation, when an organism has a life cycle very much shorter than the period of the variation there is a possibility that equilibrium either in a monospecific assemblage, or by competitive exclusion when many species are initially present, may occur before the environment changes sufficiently to influence the process.

When the life cycle is long compared with the environmental period the organism will have to be adapted to such changes, and again equilibrium may ordinarily be expected.

With intermediate lengths of life cycle, and so of time taken to achieve equilibrium, either monospecific or competitive, the equilibrium may never be achieved. In cases of annual animals with rather poor adaptation to extremes of weather but very large numbers of eggs, we are apt to have the populations being regulated primarily by extraneous or density-independent factors, so that only in exceptionally favorable circumstances does there appear to be either intraspecific or interspecific competition. The phenomenon of years of abundance and scarcity is well marked. Such cases have given rise to one whole school of animal ecologists whose leading representatives are Andrewartha and Birch.[51] Though much of their argument is of great cogency, in the long run it seems likely that competition with density-dependent regulation must occur on sufficiently frequent occasions to have a determining role in evolution.

A most cogent example of this has been given by Ford and Ford,[52] in the case of the marsh fritillary butterfly *Euphydryas aurinia*. This insect was studied in a colony occupying a small area in Cumberland, England, between 1881 and 1935. Early in the history of the colony the insect was abundant and relatively constant in pattern. After 1897 the size of the population declined; in 1917–19 only two or three specimens could be found on any one day where they had once been present by the thousands.

There was then a rapid increase in numbers so that in 1925 the original high density was restored, though a slight decline may have occurred in the succeeding decade. During the phase of increase the butterfly became remarkably variable, many extreme and deformed specimens being present. Later the extreme variants disappeared and the population settled down to a uniform type, but one differing perceptibly from that of the original population. It is obvious that during the period of increase, natural selection, and so intraspecific competition, were operating much less vigorously than later when the population was again stabilized. Wherever we have opportunistic species undergoing increase without such variability appearing, it is probable that either there is more intraspecific competition than appears, or the species has in previous episodes of natural selection become adapted to opportunistic expansion by developing low mutation rates or other genetic mechanisms reducing phenotypic variation.

51. H. G. Andrewartha and L. C. Birch, *The Distribution and Abundance of Animals*, Chicago, 1954.

52. H. D. Ford and E. B. Ford, Fluctuation in numbers and its influence on variation in *Melitaea aurinia*, *Trans. R. Entom. Soc. London*, 78:345–51, 1930. See also E. B. Ford, *Butterflies*, The New Naturalist Series, London, 1945; and *Ecological Genetics*, London, 1964.

Wherever a population is somewhat dependent on meteorological conditions and is geared in its fluctuations to an annual cycle by the life history of the species, we may expect apparent opportunism, and apparent replacement of one species by another, which in any year may indeed simulate competition, even if the species are not competitors and later may occur together in abundance. The same rather confused picture is apparent in the freshwater plankton, where it has been already suggested that failure to achieve equilibrium may be due to reversal of competition by irregular changes in external conditions. In all cases we may suspect that in contrast to conditions where life histories are very short or very long and equilibrium established in periods less than or much greater than the period of environmental change, wherever the timing of the population growth involves periods of the same order of magnitude as those of the environmental changes, there will be complexity and apparent confusion. Darlington[53] has considered the difference in life-history length between an annual plant in which selective elimination of a chromosomal irregularity can occur at once, if it produces infertility, without the involvement of a vast amount of photosynthesis and growth, and a tree in which a very large amount of growth over years and vast occupation of space must occur before any of this kind of natural selection occurs. He believes this to underlie the great cytological variation from species to species in annual herbs, while in long-lived trees such variation is too risky and chromosome numbers are apt to characterize not subspecies or species but families or even groups of families. This is a remarkable example of what differences in life history can do to evolutionary processes. It is almost certain that other unsuspected cases await to be studied.

The length of the life cycle relative to environmental change is not the only kind of relevant classification of life histories. We may also consider the competitive relationships found be-

53. C. F. Darlington, *Chromosome Botany*, London, 1956.

tween adults and their offspring. In general we may distinguish
five different types of situation.

1. The mechanism of feeding is essentially the same in adult
and juvenile, but the former being larger and the latter smaller
there is a great difference in the sizes of the food taken, so that
the adults and young can belong in different niches. In many
arthropods growth is discontinuous and the usual sorts of difference in size between instars may be about the same as between
sympatric species separated by size differences.[54]

2. The feeding mechanism is of such a kind that it grows by
adding new units which are of essentially the same size so that
adults and young differ primarily in the number of such units
and therefore eat the same-sized food. This is the characteristic
condition of sedentary aquatic animals such as sponges and
tunicates and in a less dramatic form in the colonial hydroids
and polyzoa. In all such cases, however, competition is likely
to be primarily for substrate.

3. By the introduction of various kinds of metamorphosis, the
larvae and adults feed on quite different food and so do not
compete, as in the holometabolous insects, some crustaceans
and in very early stages most marine, though not freshwater,
animals. In some cases the transitions are very extraordinary, as
in the hypermetamorphic beetles and in those butterflies, such
as *Maculinea arion,* where the late larva is carried into ants' nests
for the sake of its secretions, and after an early phytophagous
phase on wild thyme, starts feeding on ant larvae.

4. The development of various forms of parental care, or in
some invertebrates the mere production of single very large eggs
or larvae (tsetse flies), produces individuals of adult size at the
beginning of their free life, so that older adults compete with
younger of the same size, though in vertebrates not of the same
experience.

54. David C. Grant, Specific diversity in the infauna of an intertidal sand
community, Yale Ph.D. thesis (to appear initially in university microfilms).

5. The production of numerous small young as in (1), but with the adults feeding cannibalistically. This probably often happens accidentally in invertebrates and fish. In very simple communities, as in some crustaceans living under rather special circumstances,[55] this case may have some significance, the young forming the only intermediate link in the food chain between the phytoplankton and the adult.

At present it is not possible to go much further than to point out the existence of such categories, though it is clear that some of them can preadapt organisms to particular evolutionary paths. The situation in which the juvenile is launched on a free life at about the adult size obviously permits in certain cases a long period of dependent learning, and it also may lead to competitive situations in which the adults are favored by experience but in some cases the younger individuals by strength and youthful vitality. This becomes an important situation in man, particularly once the stage of conscious identity is reached.

The cases in which young and old feed in the same sort of way, but on different sized food, lead to a special situation whenever interspecific competition is moderated by size differences between the species, for here the adults of the smaller species may, if simultaneously present with the young of the larger, compete with the latter. This is likely to lead to selection in favor of timing of such a kind that all stages simultaneously present differ in size, the smaller species developing later than the larger. In a previous work[56] I have drawn attention to a possible case in the water bugs of the genus *Corixa,* and Slobodkin and Griffing[57] have given evidence of a rather widespread

55. H. Loeffler, personal communcation.

56. G. E. Hutchinson, Homage to Santa Rosalia *or* why are there so many kinds of animals? *Amer. Nat., 93*:145–59, 1959 (reprinted in *The Enchanted Voyage,* New Haven and London, 1962).

57. L. B. Slobodkin, personal communication. Since this book went to press Beatrice Vogel Durden has given me material suggesting the staggering of the life histories of three or four co-occurring corixids in Arizona.

phenomenon of the kind in microphagous pond animals, not necessarily closely related. The subject however deserves far more study. Too little attention has so far been given to the exact mechanisms by which life histories at least of the terrestrial and freshwater invertebrates are adjusted to the cycle of the seasons.

Polymorphism and niche diversity

The use of polymorphism in enabling a species to increase the size of its niche provides interesting possibilities but is only really understood in rather special cases such as those of sexual dimorphism and of polymorphic mimicry.

In the case of sexual dimorphism, in many organisms the female is larger than the male. Of course in many groups there is practically no size difference, and where aggressive and territorial behavior by the male is useful to the survival of the female and her offspring, large males or males with large weapon-like structures may occur. In many cases, however, where the male is shorter-lived and also smaller than the female, he does not compete with her during her late preadult and adult life. Where the life duration is essentially the same and both sexes play a part in insuring the success of the brood, as in the birds of prey, a considerable size difference, expressed in the falconer's term tiercel, or as a photoengraver would say, "one-third off," may permit the two sexes[58] to exploit different food niches in a way advantageous not only to themselves but to the young. Feeding differences, not involving differences in size, between the sexes are known in birds other than the birds of prey; Rand[59] quotes as examples of extremes the two in-

58. R. W. Storer, Variation in the resident sharp-shinned hawks of Mexico, *Condor, 54*:283–89, 1952.

59. A. L. Rand, Secondary sexual characters and ecological competition, *Fieldiana Zool., 34* (no. 6):65–70, 1952.

dividuals of a pair having their own feeding territory, alleged in the St. Kilda wren, *Troglodytes t. hirtensis,* and the extraordinary and supposedly symbiotic differences in bill in the extinct huia *Heterolocha acutirostris* of New Zealand.

In the invertebrates there are of course a number of extreme cases of size difference between the sexes, notably the small but structurally perfect males of a few insects, some spiders, and all Cladocera, the very reduced males of the rotifers and the small males parasitic on the females in some cirripeds, echiuroids, and parasitic isopods, with the oceanic angler fishes adding vertebrate examples. In these cases, however, the smallness of the free-living male merely reduces competition without much additional exploitation of another niche. Where the reduced male is a small parasite on the female, it is, of course, in a way, providing the advantages of both hermaphroditism and amphimixis.

Viewing the animal kingdom as a whole, however, it seems that the reduction of the male sex is far less common than might a priori have been supposed likely. In the vast majority of insects, crustaceans, and bisexual mollusks as well as in most other groups, the male, while obviously competing with the female for any limiting resources, contributes nothing but sperm to the next generation, and this could be done by a much rarer or much smaller organism, as well as by hermaphroditism. The phenomenon discussed by Fisher,[60] namely that all offspring of a bisexual species have a father and mother from which they can inherit, leads to the corollary that the possibly adaptive situation of having but a few promiscuous males in a large female population cannot ordinarily arise, since whichever sex is present at maturity in smaller numbers leaves proportionally more descendants, and in general organisms will not inherit from either sex any genetic mechanism tending to inhibit the production of that sex. Usually either bisexuality

60. R. A. Fisher, *The Genetical Theory of Natural Selection,* Oxford, 1930.

must be abandoned or the sexes must appear in about equal numbers. Reduction in size of the male might be easier, but it would probably lead, in all univoltine or paucivoltine species, to great difficulties in synchronization, the small male maturing too early. It is also not improbable that if we have great differences in size and consequently in structure, any genetic changes favorable to one sex might prove unfavorable to the other. In spite of the advantage of having reduced males, compensatory advantages in having sexes of comparable life history and comparable developmental physiology have probably rather generally operated against this type of internal niche diversification. That few of the lower vertebrates followed the oceanic angler fishes enables us, as both women and men, to regard both our parents as psychologically of equal importance, even if in different ways. This of course has been a matter of very great significance in human evolution.

The type of adaptive polymorphism that has the best explanation is that found in the more elaborate cases of mimicry. Although Jane VZ. Brower[61] has shown quite clearly that with a sufficiently distasteful model, mimicry can operate, though with a reduced efficiency, even if the mimic is commoner than the distasteful species that is mimicked, it is clear that the protection given by the false warning color of the mimic will be greater if the latter is rarer than the model. Adaptations that work best when a species is rare and fail when it is very abundant are obviously promoting survival less well than those that operate at a high density. If a mimic could become polymorphic, each form mimicking a different model, the high efficiency of the mimic could be retained in a much increased population. This is exactly what seems to have happened in say *Papilio dardanus;* from the standpoint of avoidance of predation the

61. J. VZ. Brower, Experimental studies of mimicry: *IV*, The reactions of starlings to different proportions of models and mimics, *Amer. Nat., 94*:271–82, 1960.

different females of this species may live in at least three niches. The reader is referred to Ford[62] for the genetic details of all such cases as have been studied.

It is becoming clear that the special types of situation exemplified by polymorphic mimicry, or the genetic determination of caste in bees of the genus *Melipona,* to name the best understood cases,[63] are only extreme cases of a very general adaptive polymorphism, the meaning of which is far from clear. Ford[64] in his recent *Ecological Genetics* gives an admirable discussion of the cases which he has studied for the better part of a lifetime, involving the butterfly *Maniola jurtina* and the moth *Panaxia dominula.* In both insects fairly stable polymorphic populations occur that give clear evidence of the operation of natural selection on genes determining color pattern, but in neither case is it likely that it is the color pattern that is involved in selection but rather other correlative pleiotrophic properties. In the very well-studied case of the snails of the genus *Cepaea,*[65] in which it is certain that the color pattern is of great selective significance in producing a general procrypsis, reducing predation by birds, there is nevertheless evidence of other physiological effects of the genes involved. It is therefore not very surprising to find that the biochemical and physiological polymorphism which seems characteristic of all vertebrates and many invertebrates that have been carefully studied, involves extremely significant selective effects which are no more obviously related to the known expressions of the genes than are the

62. E. B. Ford, *Ecological Genetics* (above, n. 52).

63. W. E. Kerr, Genetic determination of caste in the genus Melipona, *Genetics,* 35:143–52, 1950.

64. E. B. Ford, *Ecological Genetics* (above, n. 52).

65. See particularly A. J. Cain and P. M. Sheppard, Selection in the polymorphic land snail *Cepaea nemoralis* L., *Heredity,* 4:275–94, 1950; The effects of natural selection on body colour in the land snail *Cepaea nemoralis, Heredity,* 6:217–31, 1952; Natural selection in *Cepaea, Genetics,* 39:89–116, 1954. These researches and those of other workers, notably Lamotte, are admirably reviewed by E. B. Ford, *Ecological Genetics,* chap. 9.

selectively significant expressions of the visible polymorphs of *Maniola* or *Panaxia*. It is very likely from an ecological point of view that all species or at least all common species consist of populations adapted to more than one niche.

In most of the well-established cases it is still very difficult to understand how the environmental variables affect the polymorphism. Ford gives several extraordinary examples in *Maniola*.[66] In the spittle bug *Philaenus spumarius,* in which there are a number of color forms, the proportions vary enormously in different localities, though it is reasonably certain that at least some populations are in genetic equilibrium; one from near Cambridge, England, hardly changed significantly in over 40 years.[67] The various mutants involved must be quite old—they can occur in varying but sometimes equivalent proportions in Europe and North America; the populations in the New and Old Worlds seem to be slightly differentiated on a subspecific level by genitalia characters and so are probably old and not due to recent introductions. No obvious explanation as to why the proportions should be much the same in parts of Wisconsin and of England, but so very different in Finland, is forthcoming. In this case, as Owen and Wegert have suggested, it is possible that mere diversity is adaptive, for de Ruiter[68] has found that predators such as birds may tend to search for objects like their last meal, so that a conspecific but differently colored form might be passed over just because it was different.

---

66. E. B. Ford, *Ecological Genetics* (above, n. 52).

67. Halkko, O., Polymorphism in populations of *Philaenus spumarius* close to equilibrium, *Ann. Acad. Sci. Fennicae, 59*:1–22, 1962; Geographical, spacial and temporal variability in the balanced polymorphism of *Philaenus spumarius, Heredity, 19*:383–401, 1964; D. F. Owen and R. G. Wegert, Balanced polymorphism in the meadow spittle bug, *Philaenus spumarius, Amer. Nat., 96*:353–59, 1962; G. E. Hutchinson, A note on the polymorphism of the homopteran *Philaenus spumarius* (Linn.), *Ent. Month. Mag., 99*:175–78, 1964.

68. L. de Ruiter, Some experiments on the camouflage of stick caterpillars, *Behaviour, 4*:222–32, 1952; see also R. A. Fisher (above, n. 60).

Symbiosis among closely related species

While most members of symbiotic relationships are very un-related organisms, fungi and algae in the lichens, fungi and flowering plants in mycorhizal associations, bacteria and plants in root nodules, yeasts and insects, sea anemones and hermit crabs, and so forth, there are certain numbers of cases in which association of several closely allied species may seem to suggest some degree of symbiosis along with a greater or lesser degree of niche specificity. One of the most peculiar cases relates to the larger birds of prey of Kenya. Here Brown[69] found evidence of several species tending to live together on particular hilltops, neglecting other adjacent eminences which seemed equally suit-able. In the most striking case a single pair of each of six species of eagle occupied a hilltop, and a pair of a seventh, more low-land, species was resident not far below. Four pairs, of three species, of other birds of prey were also present. The rest of the range of hills, an area about three times the area of Eagle Hill, had but two pairs of eagles and three pairs of other birds of prey. The same phenomenon is noted in other parts of Kenya. Unfortunately the possibility of rapacious and unscrupulous collectors precluded Brown from publishing his data in detail, but it seems quite clear that a nonrandom pattern leading to interspecific but not intraspecific aggregation occurs.

For the species present on (Fig. 10) or near the hill Brown gives the following notes on food and foraging area; the wing lengths are from Mackworth-Praed and Grant,[70] who give as the principle food the item italicized in the food list, which is otherwise derived from Brown.

69. L. H. Brown, On the biology of the larger birds of prey of the Embu district, Kenya Colony, *Ibis, 94*:577–620, 1952; *95*:74–114, 1953.

70. C. W. Mackworth-Praed and C. H. B. Grant, *Birds of Eastern and Northeastern Africa*, Handbook of African Birds, ser. 1, vol. I, London, New York, and Toronto, 1952.

Aquila verreauxi *Stephanoaetus coronatus* *Polemaetus bellicosis*

Hieraaetus spilogaster *Hieraaetus dubius* *Circaetus cinereus*

Fig. 10. Six species of eagles (x 1/18) which can live together on a single mountain top in Kenya. (Adapted from all available sources by Lorraine L. Larison.)

Aquila verrauxi (wing length 569–626 mm.): *hyrax,* small antelopes, game birds, poultry; hunting mainly on rocky hills.

Stephanoaetus coronatus (wing length 458–527 mm., but in body largest species): small antelope, hyrax, *monkeys,* mongoose; hunting mainly in forest or dense bush.

Polemaetus bellicosus (wing length 553–605 mm.): *game*

birds, poultry, hyrax, small antelopes, and other mammals; hunting mainly in open country, hunts hyrax on rocky hills, raids human habitations.

Hieraaetus spilogaster (wing length 405–470 mm.): *game birds,* poultry, small mammals including hyrax, mainly in open country and farmland around human habitations.

H. dubius (=*ayresi*) (wing length 335–405 mm.): probably like *H. spilogaster,* but is a distinctly smaller species, and apparently found feeding on more rocky hills; Mackworth-Praed and Grant give *rodents,* especially squirrels, as the main food.

Aquila wahlbergi (wing length 398–455 mm.): *small mammals,* reptiles, young game birds, poultry (Mackworth-Praed and Grant add insects); hunting mostly below 1,400 m. above sea level.

Circaetes cinereus (wing length 500–555 mm.): *snakes,* game birds, poultry, occasionally *small mammals;* hunting mainly in open country.

There is clearly some degree of niche separation based on food size, and also in the kind of terrain preferred for hunting. There may also be some qualitative preferences not dependent on size or terrain. In no case is there any absolute distinction. Observation shows that there is very little interspecific aggressive behavior, though the central parts of the territories appear not to overlap. Brown, following a hint from J. G. Williams, thinks that there is a sort of balance between territoriality involving primarily intraspecific coaction and sociality involving almost exclusively interspecific coactions. Such a situation would have great theoretical interest and deserves further exploration.

Let us consider a species S_1 which obtains, owing either to structure or inherent behavior, an optimal food A, but can substitute to some extent a less easily obtained food B, in such quantities that the capture of any mixture of food between three units of A and two units of A and one of B in unit time permits a pair to rear, in the course of a lifetime, enough offspring to ensure an equilibrium population. Let us suppose a second species S_2, able to obtain the food B better than food A, so that any mixture between three units of B and two of B and one of A can insure a pair remaining part of an equilibrium population.

Consider now a site on which several birds can have nesting territory, with feeding territory extending out from the breeding site. If the feeding territory within effective cruising range can yield three units of A and three units of B, pairs of both S_1 and S_2 can maintain equilibrium populations even with some overlap in food between the species, but two pairs of S_1 cannot both successfully establish themselves, nor can two pairs of S_2. Under these conditions the optimal arrangement for either species will be strong intraspecific territoriality which will insure that two pairs do not live at the same site competing for food and probably both failing to reproduce, and a very marked interspecific toleration which ensures that all good available sites are fully used. The easiest way for the required discrimination to arise in the face of strong intraspecific territoriality might well be development of a mild attraction, at least to the extent of a pair recognizing that where another pair lived, so long as the birds of that pair were of the same general size and shape but with different recognition marks, would be a good place to live also. This type of behavior in any mathematical treatment, if it actually proved advantageous, would appear as mutual negative competition or symbiosis. If there are enough different kinds of food the argument can be generalized to any number of species. It does involve treating the populations as composed of discontinuous units of which only a few may successfully occupy a site. It is unlikely that large populations of small animals would behave in such a way.

The most extraordinary case of symbiosis within a genus is that of the periodic cicadas of the genus *Magicicada,* one of the great natural wonders of North America. Here there are three predominantly northern species with a life history of seventeen

years, *M. septendecim, M. cassini,* and *M. septendecula,* and
three equivalent more southern populations with a thirteen-
year cycle, given specific rank as *M. tredecim, M. tredecassini,*
and *M. tredecula,* by Alexander and Moore.[71] Apart from their
fantastically long life history, the remarkable thing about these
insects is that wherever they occur, broods of the species present
in any locality, usually all three of a life-cycle group, emerge
together synchronously. The only reasonable explanation is
that since the intervals between emergence are very long, no in-
crement of predators or parasitoids dependent on a particular
stage in the life history is likely to influence the amount of destruction when the same stage is reached thirteen or seventeen
years later. This situation is of course optimal if either a single
brood, or widely spaced broods, are present and all species are
synchronized, giving a minimum number of years of emergence
in a given time span. Moreover since the intervals between
emergences are prime numbers of years, resonance with shorter
cycles of set multiple numbers of years is not possible.

These two examples, one of a very marginal kind of symbiosis,
the other of a much more dramatic sort, at least suggest that
where co-occurrence of allied species provides a really puzzling
problem in terms of competition, symbiosis may actually be
occurring. In both the cases considered there is however considerable niche specificity, though in theory this might not always be the case.

71. R. D. Alexander and T. E. Moore, The evolutionary relationships of
17-year and 13-year cicadas, and three new species (Homoptera, Cicadidae,
Magicicada), *Misc. Publ. Mus. Zool.,* Univ. Michigan, *121*:1–59, 1962; M.
Lloyd and H. S. Dybas, The Periodical Cicada problem: I, Population
Ecology; II, Evolution (*in press*). The point about the significance of the
prime numbers is made parenthetically in the second of these papers; it
is one of the very few cases of a number-theoretic property, other than odd-
ness and evenness, having a possible significance in biology. I am much
indebted to Dr. Lloyd for an opportunity to see his papers with Dr. Dybas,
prior to publication.

Short-term evolutionary changes in competing populations

Pimentel and his associates[72] performed experiments in which houseflies *Musca domestica* and a blowfly *Phaenicia sericata* competed for the same limited food in a special type of population cage built of many interconnecting units, so that diffusion of the two species from opposite sides of the cage took place slowly and the effects of events on one side would not be felt on the other side of the cage for several weeks. In ordinary single-compartment cages the two species appeared nearly evenly matched and the outcome of competition experiments is apparently a matter of chance. When the experiments were conducted in the complex cage, after an initial feeble attempt on the part of the blowfly population to establish itself in the face of great increase in the houseflies, there was a sudden explosive increase in blowflies and the houseflies were enormously reduced and finally exterminated. There is evidence that in this case the rarer species, encountering its interspecific competitor far more than its own species, undergoes intense natural selection in the direction of favorable interspecific competition, which cannot happen to the other, abundant, species, any individual of which is far more likely to engage in intraspecific rather than interspecific competition. Ideally an oscillating system may be set up, and Pimental suspects that some equilibrium may be possible; whether the equilibrium, when established, can involve something other than niche diversification only future extension of this very fascinating work can show.

The niche and the biological community

It is evident that at any level in the structure of the biological community there is a set of complicated relations between

72. D. Pimentel, E. H. Feinberg, P. W. Wood, and J. T. Hayes, Selection, spatial distribution and the coexistence of competing fly species (*in press*). I am much indebted to Dr. Pimentel for a copy of this paper.

species, which probably tend to become less important as the species become less closely allied. These relations are of the kind which insure niche separation. They are probably balanced by another set of relationships expressing the fact that organisms of common ancestry are more likely to inherit a common way of life,[73] so that any two members of the class Pisces are almost certain to live in water, and any two species of the Cichlidae in warm freshwater, though we are probably justified in looking to Lake Nyasa to provide over a hundred different niches for the species of *Haplochromis* that inhabit the lake. It is obvious that the method of looking at the community in terms of niche structure, powerful though it may be, is incomplete. Some of the incompleteness is obvious; the ordering in food chains and trophic levels so important in considerations of energy flow can be considered holologically without any great consideration of individuals or species, though when these are also considered, important generalizations about stability in terms of the complexity of the community emerge. Such problems are clearly related to that of the degree to which the niche space can be subdivided. There are also scale effects; we began our survey of individual cases with the two African species of rhinoceros; when we considered birds three to five species were involved, in mollusks and insects we entered the tens. As we consider smaller and smaller organisms is there a point where the numbers of species legitimately regarded as congeneric and sympatric decrease again? This leads us to a virtually unexplored field of biology, namely the structure of microscopic associations in nature. Though the technical difficulties are very great, they could probably be solved by anyone who really wanted to compare the furry growth of diatoms on a stone in a stream with the larger-scaled patches of woodland that have about the same sort of uniformity when viewed from an airplane. Since a large association can spatially embrace the small ones in a given

73. C. B. Williams, *Patterns in the Balance of Nature and Related Problems in Quantitative Ecology,* London and New York, 1964.

locality it is bound to be more complicated, but the way in which elements of the environmental mosaic are combined to provide the properties of niches for organisms of different sizes is by no means obvious and requires far more study.[74]

Above all, the balance between the production of diversity and the occurrence of extinction, which leads to the peculiar appearance of evolution as a series of improbable victories snatched from the jaws of universal defeat, needs more consideration, for the continued production of increasing complexity seems to depend on very special conditions of the kind discussed in the first lecture, the relationship of which to the world as a whole is by no means obvious. We may here run into the region of pseudoproblems, but a pseudoproblem may always turn out to be a real problem in disguise.

III

Prolegomenon to the Study of the Descent of Man

Man is, from the standpoint of the present lectures, a large terrestrial mammal with a long life cycle, born of parents of approximately equal size and functional importance, living a protected life, free from ordinary competition with adults, at least till adolescence; genetically he is highly polymorphic. All these characteristics are shared with many other animals, but they are also not shared with all; any of them, separately or in combination, are likely to have played a decisive role in evolution.

When we try to approach the ecological niche of man we find immediately a number of peculiarities. Firstly, man has a zoogeographic range equaled only by certain easily dispersed protists and very small metazoans, mostly inhabitants of soil and

74. G. E. Hutchinson and R. H. MacArthur, A theoretical ecological model of size distributions among species of animals, *Amer. Nat.*, 93:117–25, 1959.

freshwater, and by the inevitable insect and mammalian companions that have spread with him. As is usual with any very widespread mammal, he has subspeciated extensively, the range in morphological differences between say a Norwegian, a Chinese, and a Khoisan bushman being probably greater than between any other set of subspecies of mammal. The subspecific differences relate as usual to size, pigmentation, proportions of extremities, some being, as in other mammalian cases, supposedly adaptive characters.[1] Taken over the whole range of the species, however, cultural adaptations, not involving genetic differences, have led to a greater difference in ecological niches than ordinarily occurs between families or even orders of mammals. We have, or have had, primarily carnivorous subspecies feeding on mammals or fish, primarily herbivorous subspecies feeding on a vast variety of cultivated food, and more often omnivorous subspecies, to which most readers will belong. One of the most curious features of human subspeciation, viewed from the standpoint of the mammalian taxonomist, is the tendency for a considerable degree of behavioral reproductive isolation to develop when two or more subspecies have mutually invaded a given region. This of course appears obvious, if distressing, in sociological terms; biologically it means that at least temporarily quasi-species tend to develop.

The most extraordinary case that I have ever seen was in the Nilgiri Hills of South India, about thirty years ago. The ter-

1. C. S. Coon, S. M. Garn, and J. B. Birdsell, *Races,* Springfield, Ill., 1950. T. Dobzhansky, *Mankind Evolving: The Evolution of the Human Species* (New Haven and London, 1962), contains the most modern, thoughtful, and authoritative account of many aspects of human evolution, emphasizing the little that is known, rather than the large amount that is not known but which may be suspected. In the present account I have used subspecies rather than race, which has acquired unfortunate overtones, or ethnic group, because I want to emphasize that what we see in man is essentially comparable to what occurs in other widespread mammals. Fortunately no mammalogist has been concerned with whether the dark subspecies of deer mouse found on black lava flows are superior or inferior to the white subspecies living on sandy coastal regions.

rain is very like the south of England, with rhododendron and gorse bushes. Some British officials and businessmen, unable to afford the luxury of living with servants in England, retired to the area around Ootacamund in the Nilgiris, which provided as familiar an ecological setting as much of the country south of London with a well-drained sandy soil, would have done. At the other end of the economic spectrum were the Todas, a very remarkable group of primitive people, the subject of a classical anthropological monograph by Rivers.[2] In addition, there were a number of Indian groups of various kinds likewise isolated reproductively, by predominantly religious barriers. The uninformed biologist, following only the definition of a species given in any modern work, would have made a number of species of *Homo* from the inhabitants of the region around Ootacamund.

Reproductive isolation, a good deal of morphological and behavioral divergence, and clear occupation of different ecological niches, would all be in favor of this interpretation. Quite apart from the purely practical, ethical, and sociological problems involved, it is clear that the noninterbreeding morphologically distinguishable and ecologically differentiated subgroups of man are only superficially like species, because when in the lower animals behavioral isolating mechanisms exist, we may be reasonably certain that selection against the hybrid and a tendency to the development of nonbehavioral barriers also occurs, whereas in the long run this probably does not happen in man. At least there is no evidence of its happening; an enormous number of different kinds of subspecific hybrids are known in *Homo sapiens*. It is almost as if whenever strongly marked and somewhat territorially antagonistic subspecies entered the same territory and achieved a rather uneasy symbiosis, they started acting an evolutionary play in which species appeared to originate, only to disappear when, through changes

2. W. H. R. Rivers, *The Todas*, London and New York, 1906.

in circumstance, the theatrical nature of the venture became apparent. It is indeed hard to believe that in these aspects of his behavior, man has not been influenced by and has come to imitate, albeit unconsciously, the behavior of genuine species of domestic and wild animals. The observed pattern leads to what J. S. Huxley[3] has called reticulate evolution, and in this form is characteristic of man and man alone. It is however only one aspect of the theatrical nature of human evolution.

In substituting for a process of inherited transmission of information, socially facilitated learning, a process which is significantly, though very far from exclusively, directed to passing on what one generation knows to the next, we are in one way imitating or playing genetics, so that the earliest and most recent phases of evolution have in a sense involved the development of reproducible bodies of instruction, one on how to develop, written in molecular language, the other on how to be human, composed in gestures, expressions, and ordinary spoken or written words, but at present far from perfect. These two types of transmission of information are sufficiently similar, so that not only is the molecular process usually described in linguistic terms, code, translation, transcription, redundancy, etc., but there are occasions of the greatest importance in which it is not clear what is written in the genetic molecular language and what in the behavioral organismic language. This is of course the basis of the production of quasi species just described, and therefore of some of the most important political problems facing our species as a whole. Moreover since we cannot abolish the language of genetics even if we wished to, evolutionary changes must presumably be occurring perennially in man. It

3. J. S. Huxley, *Evolution: The Modern Synthesis*, New York and London, 1942 (see p. 354). See also J. S. Huxley and A. C. Haddon, *We Europeans*, New York and London, 1936. Huxley and Haddon regard human subspecies as ideal historical constructs now intermixed to form contemporary ethnic groups; many modern systematists regard animal subspecific variation as almost as confused, but without the formation of quasi-species.

has been implicit in much of the previous lectures that various types of interaction of the organism and environment set limits, and also open up opportunities in evolution. We realize that only a fairly large animal with a fairly large brain could evolve an elaborate learning system, and that once having started to do so, the genetic transmission of inherent response mechanisms with natural selection as the only self-correcting mechanism tends to become impractical if it depends on a very large number of cell divisions with differentiation processes, at any one of which a mistake can occur. Darlington's ideas about chromosome numbers in herbs and trees may come to mind. In contrast, a learning mechanism for the elaborate responses, based on very simple inherent responses, implies a self-correcting system which acts rapidly, in a fraction of an individual's life span. Once such a system is evolved we can be reasonably certain that it will start reacting on the processes of natural selection in all sorts of unsuspected ways.

Unfortunately just as we know scandalously little about the relative importance of genetics and experience in our complicated behavior, in most cases merely being certain that both must be involved, so we also know scandalously little about human evolution as it is actually proceeding. Many people have supposed that we are tending to an edentulous, hairless condition with four toes, some have felt that intelligence must be lowered by our pattern of breeding, others that all inherited diseases for which modern medicine provides at least a palliative, must increase. These are very obvious conclusions based on a little knowledge; where deeper investigation has been possible such facile prophecies seem to lack foundation, the whole subject being far more complicated than might initially appear. There is little evidence of actual evolutionary change taking place in human populations today. There is apparently a tendency for the large-headed males and broad-nosed females in the European population of Michigan to add more to that population than do the small-headed men and long-nosed women. The level of significance of the data is however not great enough to place much confidence in the result. Clark and Spuhler,[4] who reported these observations, also found a much more significant correlation between fertility and weight or various girth measurements, but it is here uncertain whether the more pyknic individuals are inherently more fertile or whether fertility leads to a general thickening of the body.

Much more speculatively I would mention a few cases which hint at the way very complex social behavior may conceivably influence genetic evolution. These have arisen out of a number of studies by my colleague Mrs. Ursula Cowgill, who has been examining human census data for biological patterns of interest.

The first case[5] was suggested by the discovery that in a rural population in the Petén, there was a disproportionate number of adolescent boys in Maya-speaking, but not in Spanish-speaking, families. There was evidence that this could not reflect a difference in sex ratio at birth; a disproportionate number of girls must have disappeared in childhood in the Maya-speaking homes, probably dying around four years old.

A study of infantile death rates in all countries for which census data are available shows that while in prosperous, industrially developed countries the low death rate in childhood always involves more boys than girls at every age, in many less prosperous areas there is a short period around five years old when the death rate per 100 girls surviving to that period is found to be higher than the equivalent statistic for boys. This strongly suggests a tendency to neglect girls differentially in childhood, so that there is a slight impairment of general vitality and resistance to diseases. If this be so, it is obvious that

4. P. J. Clark and J. N. Spuhler, Differential fertility in relation to body dimensions, *Human Biol., 31*:121–37, 1959.

5. U. M. Cowgill and G. E. Hutchinson, Sex-ratio in childhood and the depopulation of the Petén, Guatemala, *Human Biol., 35*:90–103, 1963; Differential mortality among the sexes in childhood and its possible significance in human evolution, *Proc. Nat. Acad. Sci., 49*:425–29, 1963.

any mechanism which will counteract such a tendency will have a selective value, for the excess of boys will contribute nothing to the future population. It is suggested that the mechanism may place a selective premium on infantile sexuality, which must have a neurological basis, enabling small girls to attract more attention and nurture by flirtatious behavior than they otherwise would get. The establishment of such a hypothesis would be very difficult, but in view of the enormous psychological importance of infantile sexuality, the possibility is not without interest.

A second example from Mrs. Cowgill's study relates to the season of birth. It has long been known that there is, in many populations, great variation in the statistical distribution of births throughout the year. In contemporary Europe there is a major maximum in births in the early spring, following conceptions in early summer; in the United States the season of maximum births is now almost everywhere in September. There have been some changes in the pattern, the nature of which is not understood. One of the most dramatic discovered by Mrs. Cowgill[6] relates to Puerto Rico, where in the past twenty years the pattern has shifted from one like contemporary Europe to one like the United States. Whatever the cause of the seasonality in general, in this case the change must be cultural. Any change in birth season, except in an environment that is climatically invariant, will change slightly the kinds of risk that a newborn infant is exposed to and so tend ever so slightly to change the selective forces operating at a very critical time in the life cycle. We have no idea as to effects in this Puerto Rican case but it is fairly safe to assume that causes are operating that will have some evolutionary significance; though they might be undetectibly small, this would not necessarily be so. That such effects are possible is suggested by the very extraor-

6. U. M. Cowgill, Recent variations in the season of birth in Puerto Rico, *Proc. Nat. Acad. Sci.*, 52:1149–51, 1964.

dinary fact[7] that Bantu girls in the Transkei, born in January, February, and March experience menarche at an age on an average four months earlier than those born in November and December. Throughout the whole of childhood some physiological differences must persist between the two groups and such differences could hardly fail to be reflected in survival rates and later in fecundity as well as in the age of maturity. The matter clearly deserves rather more attention.

I mention these cases not merely because I saw the statistical work on which they are based being done and so am familiar with them, but even more because they emphasize the probably very recondite ways in which natural selection may work in man no less than in other organisms. Without some specific data the sorts of possibilities just explored would never have been considered.

Elsewhere[8] I have pointed out that there is some evidence that sexual selection, insofar as it produces evolutionary change, may operate rather differently in man and in animals, for at least in many societies, sexual display is largely a female activity, and seems to involve features, which I have termed cryptandric, based on unconscious attempts to provide the female with symbolic male genitalia. There is some reason to suspect that variation in male response to this process, which in an extreme pathological form is known as fetishism, could be correlated with variation in rates of neuropsychological maturation, perhaps involving temporal lobe function.

Another case, of enormous practical significance, may be introduced to emphasize the reconditeness of this sort of problem. It is now well known that in many societies of ultimately European origin not only has stature increased during the past

7. R. J. W. Burrell, M. J. R. Healy, and J. M. Tanner, Age at menarche in South African Bantu school girls living in the Transkei Reserve, *Human Biol.*, *33*:250–61, 1961.
8. G. E. Hutchinson, A speculative consideration of certain possible forms of sexual selection in man, *Amer. Nat.*, *93*:81–91, 1959 (reprinted in *The Enchanted Voyage*, New Haven and London, 1962, pp. 62–76).

century, but this has involved an increase in the rate of many kinds of maturation in adolescence. In Norway,[9] for instance, for which there appears to be adequate data spanning more than a century, the mean age of menarche has fallen from 17 years in 1850 to 13¾ years in 1950. Though it cannot be documented in so dramatic a form elsewhere, a considerable lowering of maturation age is apparently generally accepted by human biologists working in both Britain and America. Most non-European societies seem to exhibit the more or less contemporary European and North American pattern of relatively early menarche. It is usually believed that in the Middle Ages adolescents matured young, although not at the stature now recorded for a given age. There is evidence for a relatively constant stature in Norway in the eighteenth century, and the modal marriage age of English aristocratic girls was about a year earlier in the eighteenth than in the nineteenth century.[10] The very late maturation in the middle of the nineteenth century appears therefore to have been a special phenomenon, quite likely confined to European and derived cultures. There has been much speculation as to its cause. The favorite explanation is inadequate diet, followed by increasing diffusion of information about sound nutrition during the past century. This hardly fits the fairly early menarche observed in some underprivileged non-European groups. Initial inbreeding followed by heterosis resulting from increased mobility, due first to the development of the bicycle and then of the internal combustion engine, provides a second and truly evolutionary, if genetically rather incomplete, alternative explanation, while

9. J. M. Tanner, *Growth at Adolescence*, 2d ed. Oxford, 1962, and sources cited therein.

10. G. E. Hutchinson and U. M. Cowgill, unpublished statistical material from Debrett's peerage. L. Henry, *Anciennes Familles genevoises, Étude démographique XVI–XX siècle* (Cahier no. 26, Institut national d'études démographiques, 1956), finds the latest age of marriage among the girls of Genevan families to be in the eighteenth century. Possibly, the time of latest maturity has varied from place to place.

there is good evidence that at least growth rate can be enormously influenced by psychological factors, particularly sympathy and loving kindness at meals.[11] It is not unlikely that all three factors have been operating.

Whatever the causes, one overall effect is likely to have been an increase in sexual interest based on normal physiological processes, at the time when it is socially desirable for young people to be mainly involved in learning the extremely complicated arts of living like human beings in contemporary society. This interaction between changing physiology and educational demands, though recognized in the scientific literature, seems to have received very little attention, at least in those discussions of the problems of growing up that are most likely to influence the general public. Well-meaning people often blame the parents of wayward boys and girls for a great variety of delinquent behavior; in classical extreme delinquency, poor relations with parents may well be always involved, but in some cases of difficult adolescence it would be rather ironical if among the sins of the parents were the provision of vitamins, love, and a combination of genes that leads to a particularly rapid and vigorous ontogeny. It is obvious that no one would want to reintroduce the vitamin-poor, low-protein diets on which even the more prosperous youth in the nineteenth century was ordinarily reared, nor is the reduction of either loving kindness or heterosis likely to be any more appealing.

We clearly have to face an unexpected and in part possibly truly evolutionary change that seems to be playing havoc with our educational and moral systems. Clearly we have to reconstruct the latter so that they continue to work to produce the valuable products that they were supposed to produce in the past—broadly speaking, love of God and one's neighbor—without the disadvantages, past and present, that tend to make such systems ineffective.

11. Widdowson, quoted in G. A. Harrison, J. S. Werner, J. M. Tanner, and N. A. Barnicott, *Human Biology*, Oxford, 1964.

Even in the case of the population explosion, which is generating enough anxiety to lead to the expenditure of a little money, though a small amount compared to what is spent on other much less important matters, some of the more fundamental problems are hardly recognized. There is initially the very important psychological problem as to what sets the individually desired family size, even where family limitation is easily practiced, at a higher figure than is socially desirable. The answers are by no means self-evident, particularly when it is remembered that in the earlier part of this century in the United States family size tended to vary inversely with income but now tends to vary in the opposite way. There is a cognate practical corollary of how to supply adults with the satisfactions of large families of children and grandchildren in a stable population with a low death rate. There is an evolutionary problem as to the genetic determinants of high and low birth rates, which might have been established selectively in the past. It might be worth inquiring whether, in cultures in which expensive wedding feasts or large dowries were required, a disproportionate number of women who did not marry came from large families, a situation which would have reduced somewhat, in such communities, the otherwise inevitable selection for high fertility. If such effects could be documented it might be possible to introduce socially acceptable practices in contemporary societies giving the same effects but by quite different methods. It is also to be noted that in his present demographic state, man is comparable to Ford's marsh fritillary butterfly population in its expanding, very variable, condition. Stabilization might lead to genetic changes which in our present state of ignorance would be unpredictable and so unavoidable if not desired.

These examples are given to indicate that there are a large number of problems concerning our own species and its destiny which are too seldom thought of, let alone solved. In some cases the solution of such problems would have enormous potential practical value; in all cases, since man is the only species in

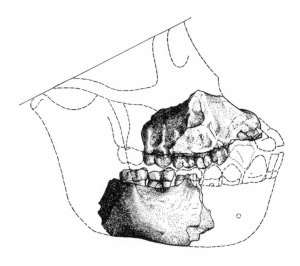

Fig. 11. Ramapithecus punjabicus mandible and maxilla with reconstruction of face (Simons).

which subjective information on desires and motivation can be obtained to correlate with more objective findings, the purely scientific interest of the investigation would be very great.

The actual historic sequence of human emergence from a primitive primate stock is beginning to become known. It is evident that the Hominidae as a family can be traced back well into the Tertiary; the Mio-Pliocene *Ramapithecus,* probably distributed from Europe south to Central Africa and east to the Punjab or farther as a single species, must be very close to our actual ancestor. At present only the face and teeth are known (Fig. 11), and have been described under a number of names. As Simons[12] has pointed out, *Dryopithecus punjabicus, Bramapithecus thorpei, Ramapithecus brevirostris, Kenyapithecus*

12. E. L. Simons, On the mandible of *Ramapithecus, Proc. Nat. Acad. Sci.,* 51:528–35, 1964.

wickeri all seem to be essentially the same organism. *Ramapithecus* is a hominid in its parabolic dental arcade, reduced canine, and in some details of tooth shape and crown pattern. We can as yet only guess as to its brain development and posture. It is most unlikely, however, to have had a cranial capacity larger than a chimpanzee, being probably a smaller animal; it may have walked more or less erect, probably picked up sticks for weapons, and may well have been less hairy than the modern great apes.[13] Between *Ramapithecus* and Leakey's[14] finds, referred to *Homo habilis,* in Olduvai bed I, there is a period of about 12 million years in which it is reasonable to suppose that the essential features of *Homo* developed, with at least some degree of speech and so an entirely new emphasis on learned behavior and the possibility of self-conscious realization that other people could be essentially like oneself. It is therefore reasonable to place in the Pliocene the beginning of man the thinking and communicating human being. Two aspects of this extraordinary evolutionary step may be mentioned specifically.

Firstly the evolution of language made possible theoretical speculation. It is impossible to ascertain when, but it certainly occurred, probably early in the history of our genus *Homo.* Today almost no known human group is without some cosmogenic theory.[15] Human beings seem to ask where they come from, a question that leads to the production of initially untestable hypotheses which in general will ultimately prove to be wrong.

Part of the history of mankind is thus the history of error. Gradually ways are found by which the previously untestable hypotheses become subject to test; as some survive the process,

13. G. E. Hutchinson, Natural selection, social organisation, hairlessness and the australopithecine canine, *Evolution, 17*:588–89, 1963.

14. L. S. B. Leakey, P. V. Tobias, and J. R. Napier, A new species of the genus Homo from Olduvai Gorge, *Nature, 202*:7–9, 1964.

15. M. Mead, personal communication, who tells me some alleged exceptions are reasonably attributed to degenerative loss.

they may become part of the general *corpus scientiarum,* or public knowledge. Other hypotheses prove to be of a different sort, being susceptible only to a kind of interior subjective test. Insofar as they can be communicated by the metaphoric use of words they become the matter of the theological basis of religion, forming, in contradistinction to the publicly testable *corpus scientiarum,* a *corpus religionis* which clearly can also undergo a refining, even if to some it would seem to lose most of its content in the process. The exact nature and interrelations of these two major kinds of human knowledge can obviously be debated; at the moment my only point is that early in their history both *corpora* would have been made up of statements almost none of which would seem acceptable today. It is very obvious that up to a point human societies are viable if most of their theoretical constructs are wrong. We clearly have a tendency, once we get the idea, to build far more theory than we need for everyday life; insofar as such theory has no bearing on our actions, it is harmless even though erroneous, but as soon as the scope of our activities increases and we enter an area involving practical issues about which we think we know something but do not, the effect is likely to be disastrous. Jane Austen's novels, particularly *Emma,* provide superb examples of the effect of wrong hypotheses in private life. Any newspaper supplies ample material for the study of false conclusions in public life. This load of error is clearly the price we pay for the evolution of intellectual penetration.

A second related point may be even more important. The initial processes of learning take place in childhood or adolescence. At first they may be very simple, but they soon involve what an ethologist would call insight, the recombination of previous perceptions leading to imaginative hypotheses.

The most important of the learning processes of *Homo sapiens,* namely the acquisition of speech, is, for everyday purposes, almost complete in childhood. The same is probably true of most elementary skills not involving the use of the full strength of the adult body. Provided the child is intelligent in learning to hear and to speak, and in a few other less complicated things, the major function of the learning process has been accomplished, and it has not very much mattered for the survival of most societies how profoundly intelligent most of the members have been in later life. In emergencies some highly intelligent leaders are no doubt often needed, but at most the demand for intellectual activity must be very small in relation to the supply available in childhood. A certain slowly acquired experience may always be desirable, but it is usually of things showing far less complex relationships than the words of sentences. For the average man the great period of intellectual activity must be over by the end of the first decade or decade and a half of life. It is reasonable to suppose that genetic selection for intellectual ability has mainly weeded out those too dull in childhood to learn their minimal cultural responses and has operated much less significantly on adult intellectual processes.

In a few societies, notably that of contemporary Uganda, there is evidence of a very early and dramatic limitation of childhood abilities[16] though initially the babies develop more rapidly than do Caucasian children over the comparable age span. This curtailment of development seems to be due in part to poor diet (kwashiorkor is common in the area), partly to a social convention requiring termination of association with the mother at weaning, and partly to institutional deficiencies, such as lack of toys in the culture. It is as yet unknown whether Ugandan children would reach a level equivalent to Caucasian if these difficulties were corrected, or whether possibly the slight initial advantage might in some ways be retained, providing ultimately a poetic retribution for much wrong done to Africa. In a more general context, the possibility of the easy inhibition of the higher types of learning is a matter of great evolutionary interest, because it may explain the extraordinary periods of

16. R. Dean and M. Gerber, The development of the African child, *Discovery*, 25:16–19, Jan. 1964.

stagnation in the development of human material culture revealed by archaeology, such as the vast period during the later Paleolithic when nothing very much seems to have been invented over a period much longer than that separating us from the foundation of the towers around Jericho, which presumably mark the beginning of urban civilization. Moreover if the process of inhibition has in some cultures a random rather than a deterministic and institutional basis, it might explain the extremely irregular development of ability even in well-educated society, though it is on general grounds very hard not to believe that some genetic mechanism involving much adaptive heterozygosity in a polygenic system is not operating also.

In essence it would seem quite likely that human intellectual development is largely an adaptation to permit young individuals to learn how to behave in a population of individuals whose behavior is unusually dependent on nongenetic information. Such a statement is of course obvious, but it does at least bring into perspective several aspects of our biology. Adult learning, insight, curiosity, and imagination appear as a paedomorphic extension of a childish set of attributes much as our large brains and short muzzles reflect the relative proportions of fetal lower mammals. The retention of certain childish characteristics that have sometimes been supposed to persist longer in highly intellectual people, along with the extreme cases of *idiot savant,* becomes more comprehensible. Initially the very gifted adult may be merely a child that has retained later than usual an intellectual attitude that has no great significance in survival. In some societies stability may have been achieved by the development of a suppressor mechanism, preventing too many dangerous ideas from disrupting the status quo. In other cases society has haltingly taken the risk of allowing some of its intelligence to develop into adult life. We have probably not yet begun to realize our full evolutionary potential in this area, which is after all the most truly human domain. We may now be entering a phase in our evolution in which failure to develop our full intellectual capacities could be disastrous, as it already is to many who drop out of school. The danger of making mistakes, inherent in the intellectual process, can moreover to a large extent be mitigated by having more and more people engaged in the process, for everyone is more likely to see other people's mistakes than his own. Behind all these possibilities there lies the truth exemplified in Marett's remark that all real progress is progress in charity.[17] As an inheritor not only of the Christian tradition but also of the empiricism of the English-speaking world, I would add that the charity is useless if it is misapplied and that the application requires immense knowledge—far more than we have today.

17. "Real progress is progress in charity," quoted by Aldous Huxley, *Ends and Means* (New York and London, 1937), on p. 7, but without reference. I have not been able to identify the quotation.

The Naturalist as Art Critic

During the early period of the formation of those large collections which ultimately became the bases of the public museums of Europe, such virtuosi and cognoscenti as collected objects of natural origin also usually collected human artifacts, both for their intrinsic value, beauty, and on account of their historic associations.

In the earliest inventory[1] of a great princely collection in Western Europe, that of the Duc de Berry, brother of Charles V of France, who was born in 1340 and died in 1416, there were a few odd natural history specimens mentioned—ostrich eggs, probably an elephant molar, tusks of wild boars, a bird's bone remarkable for its lightness, a porcupine quill, and various pebbles which seem odd in a collection made up of an unbelievable number of precious stones, pearls, jewels, vessels and images of gold and silver, and relics of the saints, almost all of which have disappeared, and of manuscripts, some of which are still among the glories of medieval French art.

Later collections, in the sixteenth century, were richer in natural history, and in fact almost exclusively biological col-

1. J. Guiffrey, *Inventaires de Jean Duc de Berry (1401–1416)*, Paris, vol. I (1894), vol. II (1896).

lections were first made at that time. However, a number of the most famous were very mixed even at a much later date. The most striking examples are those of Elias Ashmole, actually largely assembled by his friend John Tradescant, whom we commemorate in *Tradescantia,* which enriched the University of Oxford, and of Sir Hans Sloan, in part based on the cabinets of other collectors, which formed the basis of the British Museum in both its branches. Perhaps even in the seventeenth century such collections may have raised philosophical or moral problems. Jan van Kessel's painting (Frontispiece) in Florence now called "Lo Studio di un naturalista," though certainly amusing, must also have allegorical roots that I am not expert enough to excavate.[2] The naturalist whose study is depicted by van Kessel seems to have been interested in birds, caterpillars, strange and mythological plants such as the mandragora or mandrake, surveying instruments, telescopes, and coins. I would call your attention to the amount of jewelry that he amassed; this seems to have been one of the classes of object most favored by early collectors, partly no doubt as an investment as well as for its beauty.

Since we are celebrating the close of the hundred and fiftieth anniversary year of the oldest natural history museum in the United States, in a city that is also famous for its art collection,

2. In a very curious painting said to be the only known work of Giuseppe Crespi the Younger, reproduced (Plate L) and discussed (pp. 306–07) by H. W. Janson (*Apes and Ape Lore in the Middle Ages and the Renaissance,* London, 1952), a monkey is depicted holding what looks like a shell to his ear, surrounded by a fantastic assemblage of instruments, natural-history specimens, and antiquities. Janson connects this picture, from the late eighteenth century, with the *Tractatus secundus de Naturae Simia* of Robert Fludd, 1618. It now (Dec. 1964) seems far more likely that the Crespi painting, like that of J. van Kessel in the Pitti Palace, is actually part of a series, representing the five senses, displayed, at least partly, by appropriate actions of monkeys in a collector's study. *Singeries* were commonly painted in the seventeenth and eighteenth centuries; the setting of the five senses in a private museum is however an interesting and perhaps not too obvious conceit.

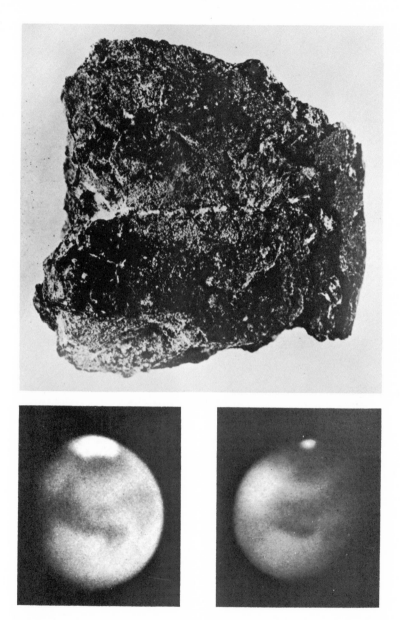

PLATE I. *Above:* Portion of the Orgueil meteorite showing vein of magnesium sulfate. *Below:* Two views of Mars, July 31 and October 8, 1956, showing the melting of a polar cap and the darkening of the dark markings, notably Pandorae Fretum, the area running a little upward to the right from the center of the disk. (After Du Fresne and Anders and after Dollfus; by permission of the University of Chicago Press.)

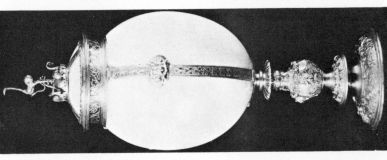

PLATE II. *Left*: Nautilus cup, Augsburg, seventeenth century; *center*: ostrich-egg goblet, Leipzig, 1560–80; *right*: *Turbo marmoratus*

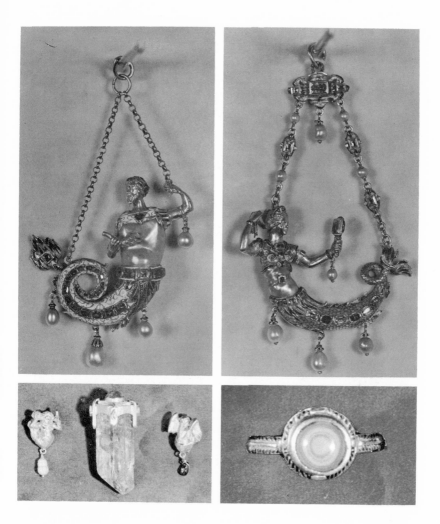

PLATE III. *Above, right:* Mermaid; *left,* triton; baroque pearls, jeweled and enameled gold, Italian, sixteenth century (Widener Coll., National Gallery of Art, Washington, D.C.).

Below, left: Topaz crystal mounted as a pin and, on either side, earrings, Mermaid in Her Vanity and Pelican in Her Piety, the former with an acorn pearl (Sah Oved, English, twentieth century); *right:* Ring, sixteenth century (Yale Univ. Art Gallery; *ex. coll.* Margaret Hutchinson, Sir Francis Cook, Marlborough, and quite possibly Thomas Howard, 2d Earl of Arundel, the greatest collector in seventeenth-century England).

PLATE IV.
Study of a Mulatto Woman,
French School 1820–25.
(By kind permission of
Fitzwilliam Museum, Cambridge.)

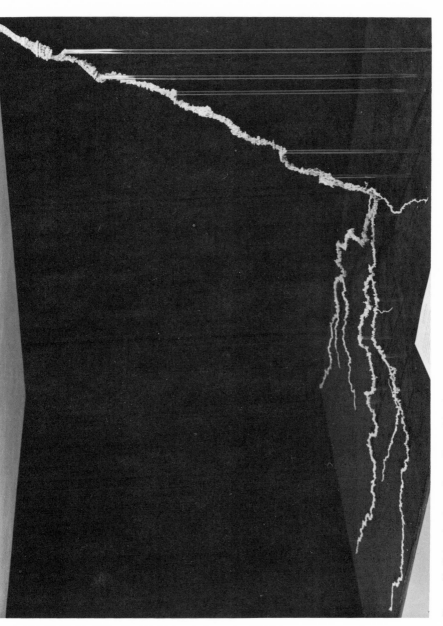

PLATE V. Fulgurite from Santa Rosa Island, near Fort Walton, Florida. (Collected and mounted by Josephine Henry, Academy of Natural Sciences, Philadelphia.)

PLATE VI. A.-H. *Abraxas grossulariata*, specimens of various forms in the collection of the Peabody Museum, Yale University. A. typical *grossulariata*, Cheshire, England; B. ab. *nigrosparsata*, Birkly, Huddersfield, bred by G. T. Porritt; C. ab. *aberdoniensis* (cf. Onslow 1919 Pl. lx, fig. 30; and·1921 pl. xix, figs. 11, 12) due to a recessive gene causing, when homozygous, a great spreading of pigment on the forewing, bred E. S. Wankin(?); D. ab. *dohrnii* bred by G. H. Raynor; E. ab. *centralipunctata* bred by G. H. Raynor, a modified and even less dark form of *dohrnii*, apparently not simply recessive or hypostatic to the latter as *dohrnii* has been bred from matings of ♂ and ♀ *centralipunctata* (Raynor pedigree in Onslow 1919); F. ab. *varleyata* bred by G. H. Raynor; G. ab. *actinota*, bred from a Yorkshire larva by W. Quibell, an extreme male form of *varleyata;* H. ab. *exquisita* bred by G. H. Raynor, apparently *dohrnii-varleyata;* I. part of the pedigreed material given by Raynor to the Zoological Museum of Cambridge University, including at the top a pair consisting of·a wild type ♂ and a *dohrnii* ♀, a granddaughter of Raynor's original specimen of 1899; the arrangement follows manuscript notes prepared by Doncaster, preserved in the drawer with a letter of Doncaster to David Sharp and a copy of Raynor's Compendium, once belonging to Francis Jenkinson and presumably added by Hugh Scott; J. forms of *A. grossulariata* reared by Onslow, and in part derived from Raynor's breeding stock, on the left at top *grossulariata*, a minor variant ab. *fulvapicata* and two rather striking variations of the black banding, *flavipalliata* with a yellow ground and *albipalliata* with a white ground, then two moderate *hazeleighensis*-like forms and finally three specimens of *lutea*, with yellow background; in center *dohrnii;* on right at top ab. *nigro-varleyata* with white band obliterated on forewing, probably actually *varleyata-hazeleighensis*, ab. *varleyata* with yellow band on forewing, two specimens of ab. *actinota* with varying white radial marks and one of ab. *leucosticta* with merely a pair of white elongate dots on the hind wing; one of ab. *exquisita* and two of ab. *pulchra*, a form with a very wide white band, unanalyzed genetically.

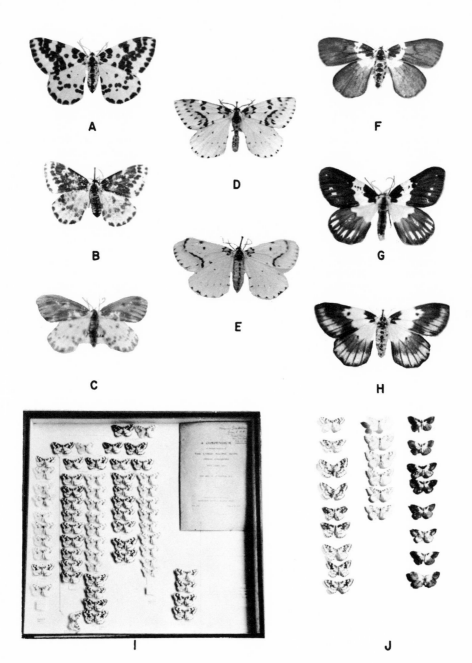

A

D

F

B

E

G

C

H

I

J

it has seemed appropriate to consider some aspects of the dichotomy between natural history and art museums, and to ask why some objects are put into one and some into the other. If at first the answers seem obvious, there will, I think, prove to be enough difficulties to lead us into interesting if obscure regions of the human mind.

Initially the objects in a collection were assembled to be looked at. They are to arouse admiration and pleasure in their beauty, wonder at their strangeness or history, envy or awe at their costliness or rarity. The simple reactions of the unlearned to the strange or marvelous give some idea of the primary reactions to objects in a collection, reactions which most of us have forgotten. A peasant woman inquires if the *Pala d'oro,* the great gold and enameled Byzantine altar frontal in San Marco in Venice, is really made of gold. Napoleon or his officials are said to have been persuaded that it was much too big to be really golden, and so left it unconfiscated and unmolested.

In the crypt of the Basilica of Sant' Ambrogio in Milan, the great Saint Ambrose lies between two somewhat undocumented martyrs, San Gervasio and San Protasio; another peasant woman exclaims "Che nomi" at hearing the unfamiliar names attached to venerable skeletons in a sacred place. In a secular context many people entering a natural history museum for the first time must wonder, if only for a moment, whether a pterodactyl or a dinosaur really could have lived, and how they got their names.

We can begin to get some insight into our problem by considering a group of rare and strange objects that achieved their greatest popularity during the period just about the time that collections were beginning to become differentiated, in which the properties of some natural object play a very great part in the decorative qualities of an objet d'art. Some of these composite objects, such as richly mounted bezoar stones or the nuts of the mysterious coco de mer *Lodoicea maldivica,* were treasured for their fancied alexipharmic properties. Most however are purely decorative and we can divide these into two more or less discrete classes. In the one that we will call *self-theorizing objects,* the natural structure that provides the decorative form also displays, or would if we fully understood it, the deterministic laws by which it came into being. Here we have an example of the effects of rotation during translation down the oviduct, in the form of an ostrich egg, mounted as a goblet (Plate II, *center*). On a much smaller scale, rotation of pearls against some more resistant part of a mollusk's foot or mantle can make an acorn pearl. This probably most often happens in mobile pearl-producing mollusks, such as the freshwater *Margaritifera* (Plate III, *below, left*). Crystals, which proclaim at least part of their atomic structure in their macroscopic shape, can be mounted in their natural condition to make jewels (Plate III, *below, left*). The banding of an agate, presumably exemplifying Liesegang phenomena of diffusion in a colloid, can be used in conjunction with the form of the bezel (Plate III, *below, right*) of a ring or any other mounting. The example illustrated, a ring dating from the sixteenth century, is of interest in that the concentrically circular agate was often regarded as a toadstone and as such protective or magical properties were ascribed to it; this ring moreover also came through Sir Francis Cook from the Marlborough Collection, which was largely formed from the jewelry of the great seventeenth-century Arundel collection. This identical ring may therefore have been in a cabinet of a great aristocratic virtuoso at the time when Jan van Kessel painted the picture we have just examined. Horns, very early made into drinking vessels, exhibit a form clearly dependent on the mode of their growth, and shells of *Nautilus* (Plate II, *left*) and *Turbo* (Plate II, *right*), used to form magnificent cups, specifically display the logarithmic spiral characteristic of the growth processes of many mollusks and some other animals.

At least in the use of shells and possibly also of more perishable materials, the employment of actual organic objects for their decorative properties and of copies of them in various workable media must have grown up side by side, giving the huge range of phytomorphic and zoomorphic forms known to art. At a more recent time wax flowers were doubtless valued for looking natural before they were valued for looking artificial.

In direct antithesis to the *self-theorizing object* may be set the *elegant inkblot,* the baroque pearl mounted to bring out its resemblance to the torso of a mythological figure (Plate III, *above*), or on a less princely scale the driftwood or other objets trouvés of the surrealists and some later schools. In these, stochastic processes dominate the form, the selection and appreciation of which obviously involves some sort of psychological projection.

In the recent history of museums the various attitudes expected to arise in the mind of the observer have been sorted out, purified, or perhaps merely divided into categories convenient in administration. We see the mixed objects that I have just described primarily as artifacts; if we happen to be interested in the pure natural history of the natural part, the artificial part is regarded as an excrescence that gets in the way of scientific vision.

Today we enter an art gallery expecting to be delighted by the beauty of certain works of man; we enter a natural history museum expecting to be instructed in the workings of nature. There are also museums in which archaeological or ethnographical material is displayed to illustrate something about man that is akin to natural history, and indeed the same point of view is apparent in the grouping of works of art in any modern art gallery, where the pictures are placed by schools and periods, i.e. geographically and chronologically, just like fossils in a paleontological collection. What seems often to be lacking, at least explicitly on the part of the intelligent public, is the realization that a number of objects in the natural history museum are of extraordinary natural beauty and that they should be valued quite simply as such, as well as for their scientific connotations. In practice in any good museum such as this one, the public displays are largely implicitly based on such aesthetic considerations. The question however of the nature of the beauty of the natural world and its relation to human art deserves more consideration than it is customarily given, and deserves such consideration quite specifically in the context of the natural history museum.

If we inquire why we make a distinction between the work of art and the object of natural beauty, which inquiry is a partial rephrasing of our original question, I suppose that at the present time the essential difference would usually be described in terms of communication or expression. What is valued in the work of art is supposedly not the sort of intrinsic beauty that we find in nature, but some evidence of a message from, or expression of, the personality of another human being, the artist who made the work. This concept however leads us into very considerable difficulties. The late Bernard Berenson said at the end of his life, of which seventy-odd years had been largely spent in problems of attribution, that it did not matter who painted a picture as long as it was a real picture. This obvious truth, coming from him, carries nonobvious overtones. In the more limited modern vocabulary that we are using, it may be rephrased that it does not matter who painted a picture as long as the picture is a genuine expression. In the light of such a statement let us look at an oil study of a mulatto lady (Plate IV) wearing only a red-and-green turban and holding a long bamboo cane, first deciding, without asking about its history, if it is a real picture genuinely expressing something to the observer.

The painting is known to have been among the effects of Eugène Delacroix, sold at auction in Paris in 1864.[3] It was ap-

3. J. W. Goodison and Denys Sutton, in *Fitzwilliam Museum Catalogue of Paintings,* vol. I, French, German and Spanish, pp. 172–74, for full discussion; also *Art News* (New York), *53* (1954), 47; *Connoisseur* (London), *133* (1954), 260; *Fitzwilliam Museum Annual Report, 1954* (Cambridge, 1955), Pl. IV, pp. 5–6. Mr. Goodison kindly writes that there can be little doubt that the attribution to Delacroix was mistaken, but that at present

parently included in a miscellaneous lot of seventeen studies supposedly by the painter himself, which were not described individually in the sale catalogue. It passed into the Cheramy Collection, and was sold, as by Delacroix, in 1908, though not listed as by him in the Cheramy catalogue published in that year. In 1954 it appeared, as by Delacroix, in an exhibition of nineteenth- and twentieth-century French painting at the Lefèvre Gallery in London. At this time it evidently generated much excitement; it was reproduced in two art journals; the *Art News,* published in New York, wrote of it as "one of the chief pleasures" of the exhibition, "amazingly forceful though only 22 inches high." It was bought from the exhibition by a leading English museum, with a subvention from the National Art Collections Fund, and at the time of the purchase was hailed as of outstanding quality and was praised for its distinction of vision and surety and sensitivity of handling. It evidently gave great satisfaction to all concerned, as it did to me when I saw it in 1958 and again in 1963. Later, however, the painting was regarded, as compared to certainly authenticated works of Delacroix's early years, "as mannered and timid in character and superficial in draughtsmanship and anatomical structure." It has indeed been suggested that it was probably the production of a dilettante called Jules-Robert Auguste, an older man who for a time knew Delacroix; on at least one occasion they both worked from the same model. Auguste's known works, in pastel rather than oil paint, are said to possess a "preciosity of vision and meticulousness of style quite in conformity" with the picture we are considering. It is very hard to avoid the feeling that great subjectivity is involved in the appreciation of such

---

the evidence is quite insufficient that the painting is by Auguste. The painting may however be compared with a known Delacroix of 1824, a portrait entitled "Aline la Mulâtresse," on extended loan to the Philadelphia Art Museum and published in their *Bulletin* of Jan. 1938 (vol. 32, no. 174).

a work: so long as it comes from the brush of M. Delacroix its virtues are emphasized; when his authorship is suspected all the faults suddenly become apparent, perhaps indeed over-apparent. This leaves us in a very difficult, though admittedly honest, position in the face of the majority of the works of art in the world, whose makers are unknown. In the case of the painting we have been considering, without being able to ex-press any real expert opinion, I have no great difficulty in be-lieving that it is not by Delacroix, but if, as seems rather un-likely, it is by a really weak painter, as Auguste seems to have been, he must have been so much under the influence of a better if younger painter when he painted the work that some of the virtues of the greater artist could be borrowed and incorporated into the work of the lesser man. It is worth noting that some-times supposedly most characteristic works of major masters have turned out, as scholarship progresses, to be copies, studio pieces, or even works of fairly independent pupils. Since in some cases only the more obvious qualities of the master may be caught and transferred to the derivative work, the latter may become a sort of elementary introduction to the subtleties of the master, with an immediate appeal leading in the right direction. The painting which first gave me insight into Zurbarán, for instance, is a Santa Rufina now believed to emanate from his studio but not from his hand. At any rate all of us who have frequented art collections for any length of time must realize that we have almost certainly got what seems to be pleasure of the very highest order out of works of suspect attribution. The exact origin of the message conveyed is perhaps of less impor-tance than is often believed.

We may now as naturalists raise a still more awkward prob-lem, one that was adumbrated by the *singerie* painters of the seventeenth century,[4] the problem of the ape as artist. Un-

---

4. For a series of seventeenth- and eighteenth-century satiric paintings of the ape as artist see Janson, chap. X.

fortunately a certain amount of inevitable commercialism and humor has tended to obscure the extraordinary significance of the work that was started fifty years ago by Kohts in Russia and which has been recently greatly developed by many workers, of whose studies Desmond Morris has provided an illuminating synthesis.[5]

The great apes and some other primates, notably capuchin monkeys, when put into an experimental environment in which they can exhibit it, have a sense of symmetry in design, which is most easily demonstrated by giving the animal a paper, blank except for a square set eccentrically. In a highly significant number of cases the animal will tend to mark the paper in such a way as to balance the design. Rensch, moreover, in experiments in which animals can make choice of ready-made designs, finds that balanced patterns pleasing to ourselves also seem to please many other vertebrates. When the animal is given more elaborate opportunities for artistic expression, Morris concludes that in all cases there is, as well as compositional control of balance, an attempt at calligraphic differentiation of line; thematic variation within an individual style appears when paintings of the same animal are compared. There is also an attempt to achieve a degree of optimum heterogeneity giving a sense that a painting is complete. At least in young apes the activity is highly self-rewarding or autotelic. Any intrusion is resented more than if the animal had for instance been disturbed when eating. Providing the young ape with paints, brushes, and canvas gives it, for the first time in its life, something very important to do.

The general level of achievement, though compared to action painting or abstract expressionism by some critics, appears to be that of a three-year-old child just prior to the development of diagrammatic representation of the human face.

What these studies show clearly is that the desire and capacity

5. Desmond Morris, *The Biology of Art*, London, 1961.

to engage in some sort of self-expressive autotelic activity exists in animals that have diverged from the human line many millions of years ago and do not have the intellectual capacity to invent the mechanisms to provide the sort of satisfaction that is within their intellectual range.

Other examples of animals being able to gain satisfaction from far more complicated types of behavior than they can invent in nature could be multiplied, though none I think are more interesting than the artistic activities of primates. The capacity of seals to learn to perform on musical instruments and in some cases to get enjoyment from doing so, is perhaps another example; here we may suspect that an interest in the rhythmical sounds of breaking waves on the rocks or beaches of a shoreline has some initial adaptive value. It is evident that in a sense the more highly developed mammals are preadapted to inventions that for most of them have not become available.

It is reasonably certain that a large part of human intellectual evolution must have consisted in the rare invention of such activities—painting, dancing, music, games, counting, and elaboration of language—which, once they had been achieved accidentally or by exceptional insight of a genius, caught on with a large part of, if not the whole, population.

Whatever the expressiveness that is required to put an object in an art gallery may be, it is clearly not quite confined to the genus *Homo;* as the evolutionist would expect, it has a history and this history can be traced outside our own genus or family.

If we are prepared to grant that at least some of the qualities present in a human painting are also present in a very rudimentary form in those of the great apes, we may legitimately inquire about certain other kinds of animal activity that seem to us to have aesthetic properties. Most conspicuous are the songs and displays of many birds, the latter perhaps culminating in the extraordinary activity of bower birds in collecting and arranging decorative objects. We may in the present state of knowledge make the following statements about such activities.

They are all parts of adaptive behavior directed to ends that are significant in the life of the animal, notably the holding of territory, retention of interest in a mate, and the like. The significance always implies some sort of social interaction. Though usually both innate and learned behavior are involved, in many cases the behavior has a stereotyped innate component that is largely lacking when a human being sings, dances, or paints, and for that matter when an ape is given the chance to do the last named. There is often a great discharge of neuro-muscular activity which is reasonably regarded as comparable to what we know subjectively as emotion.

In a very large number of cases, structures or activities used as social signals of a visual or auditory kind are found to be aesthetically significant to human beings. Apart from the fact that in many cases the activities involved are largely innate, which allies them perhaps more to elaborately grown structure than to learned activity, the social and emotional aspects of animal display and the activities involved in the production of much so-called primitive art appear to be comparable. In both cases the aesthetic elements which we value are originally secondary to the social functions subsumed by displays or rituals. If we compare the voice of a peacock with his tail we get a clear hint that what is needed to produce the secondary aesthetic effect is a considerable degree of elaboration. In all structures used in display, the elaboration is no doubt correlated with the need for quite specific signals different from anything else. The greater the elaboration of two structures the less the probability that they will resemble each other. Moreover, if we look at all the organisms which we at first sight would regard as strikingly beautiful in a decorative rather than a purely functional way, or for that matter inanimate structures which give the same sort of impression, we find that nearly all the extraordinary cases are the product of some sort of differentiation in a relatively free environment, in water, or growing up into the air or at least moving about above the ground, rather than burrowing in sand or mud. I give no illustrative material: within a major natural history museum, *si exemplum quaeres, circumspice*. Wherever there is a physical possibility of developing, in a spatially unrestricted way, in a context which either calls for or merely permits elaboration, we get natural beauty. Moreover in all cases we have more than a hint of what I initially referred to as a self-theorizing property. The elaborate form tends to express deterministic laws that brought it into being, though often we may not know what they are but merely feel that the symmetry and elegance of the object before us implies a symmetry and elegance in the theory describing its genesis.

We have seen how the random irregularities of what I have called elegant inkblots are the vehicles for certain sorts of psychological projection, entirely irrelevant to the nature of the object, yet capable of giving considerable satisfaction under certain circumstances. We have seen also how in looking at an entirely conventional human work of art there can be an enormous subjective element in evaluation; a study of either forgeries or fashions in appreciation no less than overenthusiastic attributions would lead to a comparable conclusion. We have to go out to meet the work of art on some ground between it and ourselves to receive its message; the place where we stand may make all the difference.

We have further seen that there is apparently a continuum from conscious human works of art, through immensely beautiful but in purpose only secondarily artistic works of primitive art, to animal activities and structures employed socially and then to those that are not so employed, and so finally to inanimate structures which we recognize as beautiful. As we get further from the human work, we find that what we see as beautiful comes into being largely as elaboration in a relatively unrestricted space, whatever the actual mechanisms of its development. This happens because there are orderly processes occurring in nature and when they get a chance to show what they can do, they produce elaborate works in which symmetry and elegance in the external world suggest that, even if we cannot explain the process yet, and we often can, the explanation would involve elegant theory, which it often does.

Again as with human works, our viewpoint makes a considerable difference. An unforced feeling for how a form may arise can enhance its natural beauty. Some people may be willing to stop at this point, as every philosophical position, or lack of position, implies enormous difficulties. Others may want to go on further, feeling themselves in the presence of a message from nature or the external world which they go out to meet with their understanding. To be meaningful such a position would have, I think, to be theistic. It does not involve any logically compelling argument for the existence of God, but like each of the arguments on this matter, it makes its point if one is prepared to accept some of the others.

Meanwhile I think that if the general trend of my line of thought makes at least partial sense, we can agree that in large measure the public exhibits in a good natural history museum are in some ways the modern counterparts of the nautilus cups and ostrich-egg goblets of the Renaissance, constructed of both natural objects and a highly skilled kind of applied art. Yet they are far more important, because they are made to contain not wine, which anyway would be hard to drink from such objects, but scientific truths, made plain by the art with which the self-theorizing properties of the specimens are exhibited. If the whole aspect of the work of a natural history museum is considered in this light, a taxonomically arranged set of diatom slides or a drawer of insects, no less than a habitat group or the magnificent fulgurite of Plate V are seen to have some of the properties of works of arts. Although I think there are good reasons for separating art galleries and natural history museums, they still, even after more than a century and a half of autonomous development, may have much in common.[6]

6. I am much indebted to the Soprintendenza alle Gallerie, Florence, to Dr. Erwin M. Auer, Director of the Kunsthistorisches Museum, Vienna, to Mr. J. W. Goodison of the Fitzwilliam Museum, Cambridge, and the Director of the National Gallery of Art, Washington, for permission to publish the photographs reproduced in the Frontispiece, Plate II, Plate III, *above*, and Plate IV; to Mr. Emiddio DeCusati and the Yale Art Gallery for Plate III; and to Dr. Ruth Patrick and the Academy of Natural Sciences of Philadelphia for Plate V. I am most grateful to Sah Oved (Mrs. Hughes) and Professor Charles Seymour, Jr., for assistance and information about several objects discussed, to Miss Yemaiel Oved for one of the ideas that I have used, and to my wife for much help.

The Lacustrine Microcosm Reconsidered

The great intellectual fascination of limnology lies in the comparative study of a great number of systems, each having some resemblance to the others and also many differences. Such a point of view presupposes that each lake can in fact be treated as at least a partly isolated system.

Today[1] I want to begin by considering two rather different approaches implicit in such treatment, partly in the work of Birge and Juday during the time when they were making Lake Mendota famous throughout the scientific world, and partly in the earlier work of S. A. Forbes, from whom my title is of course derived.

Birge's mature point of view is expressed in his concept of the heat budget,[2] which, though derived from ideas of Forel and others, represented a highly original and important contribution because it first called attention to the lake as a natural system with an input and an output. This point of view has

1. Text of address given after the transfer of keys of the Laboratory of Limnology from the National Science Foundation to the Board of Regents of the University of Wisconsin, at Wisconsin Center Auditorium, Madison, May 8, 1964. The author on this occasion represented the International Association for Pure and Applied Limnology.

2. E. A. Birge, The heat budgets of American and European lakes, *Trans. Wis. Acad. Sci. Arts Lett.*, 18:166–213, 1915.

tended to underlie most of what has been done in lake chemistry and in the study of primary productivity during the past three or four decades. Such a way of thinking, in which the lake is considered, in the jargon of the moment, as a black box, has been called elsewhere[3] the *holological* approach. It has been extremely fertile, but, since water is transparent, the black box is too restrictive an analogy. The time has perhaps come for further development of the antithetical *merological* approach, in which we discourse on the parts of the system and try to build up the whole from them. This is what Forbes was trying to do in his classical lecture on "The Lake as a Microcosm."[4]

It is desirable to think for a moment about certain scale effects characterizing the lacustrine microcosm when viewed by a human observer. If we suppose that an organism reproduces about once every week in the warmer half of the year and on an average about once every month in the cooler half, it will have about thirty generations a year. This corresponds in time to about a millennium of human generations, and considerably longer for those of forest trees. In the case of the latter, we should expect in thirty generations some secular climatic change to be apparent. We should not expect in a tree the seeds or resting stages to remain viable while thirty generations passed, and in the larger animals no such stages exist. The year of a cladoceran or a chrysomonad, in both of which groups rapid reproduction may alternate with the formation of resting stages, is thus in some ways comparable to a large segment of postglacial time, though in other ways the comparison either to several millennia, or to a year in the life of a human being or tree, is definitely misleading. Another peculiar scale effect is that, in passing from the surface to the bottom of a stratified lake in summer, we can easily traverse in 10 to 20 m. a range of physical

3. G. E. Hutchinson, Food, time and culture, *Trans. New York Acad. Sci.*, ser. II, 5:152–54, 1943.
4. S. A. Forbes, The lake as a microcosm, *Bull. Scient. Assoc. Peoria*, 1887:77–87, reprinted, *Illinois Nat. Hist. Surv.*, 15:537–50, 1925.

and chemical conditions as great or greater than would be encountered in climbing up a hundred times that vertical range on a mountain.

I would also emphasize how fantastically complicated the lacustrine microcosm is likely to be. There is probably no almost complete list of species of animals and plants available for any lake, but it would seem likely from the several hundred species of diatoms and of insects[5] known from certain lakes that a species list of the order of a thousand entries may be not unusual. This probably means that in the course of a season at least a thousand somewhat different ecological niches may for a time be recognizable. Most of this diversity is associated with the shallow marginal waters in which the bottom can form a solid substratum for attached aquatic plants.

Simpler situations in a lake are probably provided by the plankton, though it soon appears that they are not particularly simple and that we cannot regard the plankton, excluding the rest of the community, as an entirely satisfactory entity. We begin with the variously named and deductively respectable principle that two co-occurring organisms cannot form equilibrium populations in the same niche. In the phytoplankton we immediately meet the paradoxical situation of an enormously complicated association of phototrophic species all living together under conditions that do not seem to permit much niche specialization.

It is possible that the permanent and apparently almost monospecific *Anacystis* blooms recorded[6] under some conditions

5. N. Foged (On the diatom flora of some Funen lakes, *Folia Limnol. Scand.*, no. 6, 75 pp., 1954) lists up to 260 different diatom taxa from a single lake. L. Brundin (Chironomiden und andere Bodentiere der südschwedischen Urgebirgsseen, *Inst. Freshwater Res.*, Drottningholm, rep. 30, 914 pp., 1949) finds up to 140 species of insects of the family Tendipedidae in a single lake.

6. S. V. Ganapati, The ecology of a temple tank containing a permanent bloom of Microcystis aeruginosa (Kutz) Henfr. I., *Bombay Nat. Hist. Soc.*, 42:65–77, 1940; G. E. Hutchinson, The paradox of the plankton, *Amer. Nat.*, 98:132–46, 1961.

in tropical waters, notably temple tanks of South India, may represent a monospecific equilibrium of the kind to be expected from theory. Much more often, what I have elsewhere termed the paradox of the plankton intrudes itself. It is to be noticed that the paradox of a multispecific phototrophic phytoplankton only arises if we assume a closed system, providing a single niche, with enough time to permit the achievement of equilibrium. In general in a lake, we do not have a single niche system that is closed. The epilimnion if reasonably turbulent may approach a single niche system, but introductions from the littoral benthos are always possible. Moreover, there is no rule about the speed at which competitive exclusion excludes. As Hardin[7] has pointed out, in the theory all that is needed is an axiom which states that no two natural objects, or classes of objects, are ever exactly alike. What then happens is that under constant conditions one class, or population of reproducing objects, finally displaces the others. If the conditions are continually changing, the favored species might also change. This is what usually seems to be happening, but it must not be forgotten that a multispecific system never in equilibrium would be expected to suffer continual random extinctions and, if not quite closed, random reintroductions also, and should therefore drift in specific composition, probably more than is indicated by paleolimnological data.

It is possible that, in a lake, random extinction is primarily a danger for the rarer species which are never likely to be observed. In a square basin 1,000 m. across and 1 m. deep we should have 10^6 organisms so common that one occurred per cubic meter, 10^9 of those occurring a thousand times more often at a rate of one per liter, and 10^{12} of those with one individual in the average cubic centimeter. If we are considering ordinary phytoplankton organisms, the first organism would be far too

7. G. Hardin, The competitive exclusion principle, *Science, 131*:1292–97, 1960.

rare ever to find by ordinary techniques even though the population before us numbered a million.

I am now inclined to think that a large part of the diversity of the phytoplankton is in fact due to a failure ever to attain equilibrium so that the direction of competition is continually reversed by environmental changes, as suggested many years ago, moderated in two ways which insure that competitive exclusion does not continually and irreversibly remove bits of the association. The first moderating influence is the speed at which exclusion occurs. In spite of the ultimate validity of Hardin's axiom of inequality, Riley[8] feels that a sort of asymptotic approach to more or less equal adaptation is not unexpected in the phytoplankton. If we suppose two species S_1 and S_2, such that in niche N_1, S_1 displaces S_2, and in niche N_2, S_2 displaces S_1. Seasonal environmental changes now occur, so that at first only N_1 and then N_2 are available. If competition went fast compared with the rate of environmental change, S_1 would be eliminated and would not be available for a new cycle, but if the two species were almost equally efficient over a wide range of environmental variables, competitive exclusion would be a slow process. Both species then might oscillate in varying numbers, but persist almost indefinitely.

The second way of moderating the tendency to random extinction is the provision of resting stages, so that if S_1 is eliminated completely as an active competitor in the plankton, when N_1 gives place to N_2, later next season when the reverse change occurs, resting stages of S_1 can recolonize the environment now again providing niche N_1. In practice any plankter that really disappears and reappears rather than becoming alternatively rare or very common must have some such stages. Annual macrophytes and many small animals also have such stages as seeds, eggs, pupae, and the like. Perennials, moreover,

8. G. A. Riley, in *Marine Biology I, Proc. First Internat. Interdisciplinary Conf. on Marine Biol.*, Amer. Inst. Biol. Sci., Washington, D.C., 1963 (see pp. 69–70).

may hibernate in ways that take the individual out of competition. In the diatoms in many of which resting zygospores are still unknown, it is possibly relatively unmodified littoral or shallow-water benthic individuals that are involved in tiding the planktonic populations over competitively unfavorable conditions. In *Melosira,* Lund's beautiful work[9] shows how a relatively heavy diatom rests on the bottom for very long periods in a more or less unassimilative form; here there is doubtless some special physiological adaptation, so we are halfway between a species invading the plankton casually with a continuous littoral population and the condition in which morphologically specialized resting stages or cysts are produced. One of the most remarkable results of several recent paleolimnological studies, notably Nygaard[10] on Store Gribsø and our own work on Lago di Monterosi,[11] is the fantastic variety of chrysophycean cysts recognizable in the sediments, at least, of rather soft-water lakes. Resting stages of all sorts are of course particularly prone to occur in freshwater organisms, where they were doubtless developed primarily to promote survival under extreme physical conditions, notably desiccation and freezing. Once developed, they would however clearly be of great value in obviating extinction when conditions changed in favor of a competitor. It is therefore peculiar that Lund finds that planktonic desmids tend to lose such stages.

The diversity of the phytoplankton is clearly of primary importance in producing that of the zooplankton. Given the diversity of the phytoplankton, and some degree of food specificity in the animal forms, no striking paradoxical situation need

9. J. W. G. Lund, The seasonal cycle of the plankton diatom, *Melosira italica* (Ehr.) Kütz. subsp. *subarctica* o. Müll., *J. Ecol.,* *42*:151–79, 1954. Further observations on the seasonal cycle of *Melosira italica* (Ehr.) Kütz subsp. *subarctica* o. Müll., *J. Ecol.,* *43*:90–102, 1955. See also his Baldi lecture, *Verh. int. Ver. Limnol.,* *15*:37–56, 1964.

10. G. Nygaard, in K. Berg and I. C. Petersen, Studies on the humic acid Lake Gribsø., *Fol. Limnol. Scand.,* no. 8 (1956), 273 pp.

11. Elaine Leventhal, ms., to appear in a series of papers on this locality.

arise. Moreover, it is clear from all the available work on the seasonal succession of closely allied forms, such as the species of *Daphnia*, from Birge's[12] early studies on Mendota up to the very beautiful and elaborate investigations of Dr. J. L. Brooks and of Dr. Donald W. Tappa at Yale, shortly to be published, that the same sorts of seasonal phenomena that damp competition in plants also occur in animals.

MacArthur and Levins[13] have recently pointed out that two rather different extreme types of diversity between closely allied sympatric species (i.e. members of a genus or subfamily) are possible.

The two species may be specialized in such a way that they eat slightly different food, but hunt it over the same area. In this case morphological specializations, of which the simplest is a size difference, are to be expected. Probable examples, such as the hairy and downy woodpeckers, easily come to mind.

If the two species eat the same sorts of diversified food, they are likely to differ in the proportions in which they encounter it, and to specialize in habitat preferences without much morphological specialization becoming necessarily involved in feeding activity. MacArthur's own work on the American warblers provides a striking example. The existence of these two general situations has long been known, but MacArthur and Levins provide a good abstract theory of the phenomenon.

Over the whole vertical column in a stratified lake, even if only 10 m. deep, habitat differences are available in summer at least as great as over the range from the bottom and to the top of a mountain several hundred times that vertical range. In the turbulent epilimnion it is in general hard to develop habitat preferences and, within any layer in which free movement is habitual, size differences may be expected as the simplest special-

12. E. A. Birge, Plankton studies on Lake Mendota: *II*, The Crustacea of the plankton from July 1894, to December 1896, *Trans. Wis. Acad. Arts Sci. Lett.*, 1898.

13. R. H. MacArthur and Richard Levins, *Proc. Nat. Acad. Sci.*, June 1964.

ization increasing diversity, as is the case with Copepoda. In view of the extreme vertical variation when we leave a turbulent, freely mixed layer, the antithetic habitat difference type of specialization in the plankton is likely to be rather different from what is found terrestrially, involving fairly complete adaptation to very divergent physical factors rather than habitat preferences, though, in two species living together with vertical migration over partly overlapping ranges, we have the lacustrine analogue of birds feeding in different parts of the same tree. The rapid production of a number of generations per year permits a kind of seasonal succession in rotifers and Cladocera, though to a less extent in Copepoda, that is comparable to that in the phytoplankton. Considerable possibility of avoiding competitive exclusion is thus achieved by slow competition between species that have slightly different optima, and so succeed each other in time. Here the production of resting stages is of the greatest importance. That they are produced at the time of maximum population fits reasonably into this scheme quite independently of adaptation to unfavorable physical situations.

This succession in time may be coupled with size differences and habitat differences, probably producing, in for instance the genus *Polyarthra*[14] where five or six species can be sympatric but not always strictly synchronic, a very pronounced niche specificity.

An interesting question arises, namely to what extent sympatric species of a given taxon, say genus or family, not merely have different ecologies, but also have ecologies that, though different, are closer than any would be likely to be to that of a sympatric nonmember of the taxon picked at random.

If we compare a desert assemblage with a limnoplanktonic one, it is obvious that, if the first organism captured in the

14. Carlin, Die Planktonrotatorien des Motalaström: zur Taxonomie und Ökologie der Planktonrotatorien, *Meddel. Lunds Univ. Limnol. Inst.*, no. 5 (1943), 255 pp.

desert is a beetle, the probability that the next one of another species is also another beetle is higher than that it is a rotifer, and vice versa. It is however rather surprising to find in Carlin's data four unallied perennial rotifers, including the microphagous sedimenters *Keratella, Notholca,* and *Conochilus* and the selective predator *Asplanchna,* all reacting similarly to an unidentified difference, possibly involving an earlier decline in the late summer bloom of *Oscillatoria,* that distinguished 1940 from the other years of his study.

The relatively small development that has been possible in the study of the interrelationships of the plankton since Forbes wrote in 1887 and Birge in 1898, and of which some examples have just been given, has been due to a very large amount of work both in field observations, in very meticulous taxonomy, and in ecological theory. In the other parts of the lacustrine community the problems are more difficult though their solutions would have great fascination, as will be apparent from a single example. It we examine the lasion, "Aufwuchs" or fouling community of fresh waters, we find a variety of filamentous algae and diatoms with an associated fauna ordinarily of small motile forms. The biomass of the animals is doubtless ordinarily much less than that of plants, and on a surface near the bottom of the euphotic zone organisms will tend to be scarce. There may be a few sponges and bryozoans but they are not conspicuously important. In the sea, the parallel community, though largely algal in the tidal range, consists at most levels of an astonishing mass and variety of sessile animals—sponges, mollusks such as *Mytilus,* numerous hydroids, Bryozoa, and tunicates. The difference is presumably due to the lack of pelagic larvae other than copepodan nauplii in fresh water. The only exceptions are a very few mollusks of far from worldwide distribution, notably *Dreissena* and to a less extent *Corbicula,* the larval colonies of phylactolaematous Bryozoa, hardly ever noted in open water, perhaps a few transitory planula larvae (*Cordylophora, Limnocnida, Craspedacusta*), and the free-swimming larvae of trematodes which show odd diversity in behavior when allied species are compared, but which presumably do not enter into competition with other plankters. This is a very poor showing compared to the dozen phyla likely to be found in any series of marine neritic plankton samples. This difference has received various explanations, the most reasonable, essentially due to Needham,[15] probably being the difficulty that a small larval animal in freshwater, feeding on plant cells low in sodium and chloride, would have in acquiring enough salt before it could develop salt-absorbing organs. In a certain sense the adult animals of the marine littoral benthos, not all sessile nor all microphagous, are the resting stages removed from competition at least in the open-water plankton. We see in this type of relation a rather large-scale example of the sort of interaction which fascinated Forbes. It is hard, in reading Forbes on "The Lake as a Microcosm," to prevent the mind drifting back to the tangled bank of the last chapter of Darwin's *Origin of Species,*[16] and from there it is permissible, at least

15. J. Needham, On the penetration of marine organisms into freshwater, *Biol. Zbl., 50:*504–09, 1930.

16. The concluding paragraphs of Forbes' essay and of the *Origin of Species* may be profitably compared:

"Have these facts and ideas, derived from a study of our aquatic microcosm, any general application on a higher plane? We have here an example of the triumphant beneficence of the laws of life applied to conditions seemingly the most unfavorable possible for any mutually helpful adjustment. In this lake, where competitions are fierce and continuous beyond any parallel in the worst period of human history; where they take hold, not on goods of life merely, but always upon life itself; where mercy and charity and sympathy and magnanimity and all the virtues are utterly unknown; where robbery and murder and the deadly tyranny of strength over weakness are the unvarying rule; where what we call wrong-doing is always triumphant, and what we call goodness would be immediately fatal to its possessor—even here, out of these hard conditions, an order has been evolved which is the best conceivable without a total change in the conditions themselves; an equilibrium has been reached and is steadily maintained that actually accomplishes for all the parties involved the greatest good which the circumstances will at all permit. In a system where life is the universal good, but the destruction of life the well-nigh universal

in 1964, to look back still farther, remembering what Jane Austen said about Shakespeare, to that other "bank where the wild thyme blows."[17] Both Forbes and Darwin realize struggle but see that it has produced harmony. Today perhaps we can see just a little more. The harmony clearly involves great

---

occupation, an order has spontaneously arisen which constantly tends to maintain life at the highest limit—a limit far higher, in fact, with respect to both quality and quantity, than would be possible in the absence of this destructive conflict. Is there not, in this reflection, solid ground for a belief in the final beneficence of the laws of organic nature? If the system of life is such that a harmonious balance of conflicting interests has been reached where every element is either hostile or indifferent to every other, may we not trust much to the outcome where, as in human affairs, the spontaneous adjustments of nature are aided by intelligent effort, by sympathy, and by self-sacrifice?" (Forbes)

"It is interesting to contemplate a tangled bank, clothed with many plants of many kinds, with birds singing on the bushes, with various insects flitting about, and with worms crawling through the damp earth, and to reflect that these elaborately constructed forms, so different from each other, and dependent upon each other in so complex a manner, have all been produced by laws acting around us. These laws, taken in the largest sense, being Growth with Reproduction; Inheritance which is almost implied by reproduction; Variability from the indirect and direct action of the conditions of life, and from use and disuse: a Ratio of Increase so high as to lead to a Struggle for Life, and as a consequence to Natural Selection, entailing Divergence of Character and the Extinction of less-improved forms. Thus, from the war of nature, from famine and death, the most exalted object which we are capable of conceiving, namely, the production of the higher animals, directly follows. There is grandeur in this view of life, with its several powers, having been originally breathed by the Creator into a few forms or into one; and that, whilst this planet has gone cycling on according to the fixed law of gravity, from so simple a beginning endless forms most beautiful and most wonderful have been, and are being evolved." (Darwin)

17. I know a bank where the wild thyme blows,
Where oxlips and the nodding violet grows;
Quite over-canopied with luscious woodbine
With sweet muskroses, and with eglantine.
There sleeps Titania sometime of the night,
Lull'd in these flowers with dances and delight;
And there the snake throws her enamell'd skin,
Weed wide enough to wrap a fairy in.
A Midsummer Night's Dream
II.1.249–56.

diversity, and we now know, in the entire range from subatomic particles to human artifacts, that every level is surprisingly diverse. We cannot say whether this is a significant property of the universe; without the model of a less diverse universe, a legitimate but fortunately unrealized alternative, we cannot understand the problem. We can, however, feel the possibility of something important here, appreciate the diversity, and learn to treat it properly.[18]

18. The evening program ended with a performance of Mozart's Quartet in G Minor for Piano and Strings, K. 478.

The Cream in the Gooseberry Fool

The Reverend Gilbert Henry Raynor, who was born in 1854 and died in 1929, spent a quarter of a century, and a third of his life, as rector of Hazeleigh, a small village near Maldon, in Essex. He is known today almost exclusively as an ardent collector of Lepidoptera, and apart from such activities, it is hard to learn much of him from what has been published. His two obituary notices in entomological journals emphasize his genial and helpful disposition, and it is by his helpfulness as much as by his skill as a lepidopterist that he achieved a small but definite place in the history of science. Fortunately, through the kindness of the Reverend C. G. Bartle, rector of the now combined parishes of Woodham Mortimer and Hazeleigh, Miss C. Evelyn Croxon, who knew Raynor well, prepared a manuscript account which she generously sent to me. She writes:

> He was a kind friend to all his parishioners in their joys and sorrows; he had a ready wit and a keen sense of humor. His interests were wide and varied. His garden contained a wonderful collection of rare plants, bulbs and shrubs, and he was never tired of showing them, and explaining their origin to his friends . . . He was also a collector of old china.

A peep into his study would reveal the life cycle of many rare butterflies and moths, which he bred with much success. As a child I was often instructed by him to collect caterpillars from various plants and shrubs, and I remember being rebuked by my mother for getting a rash on my hands from handling some of these creatures, but I felt nevertheless that it had all been very worthwhile!

How right Miss Croxon was. She continues: "Mr. Raynor was a keen cricketer and tennis player, and he gave much help and inspiration to young people in their games." He clearly made the rectory at Hazeleigh a center of civilization for his small village during the quarter century of his incumbency.

Apart from this picture of Raynor in his prime, his friends C. R. N. Burrows[1] and N. D. Riley[2] record that his interest in natural history developed early; at sixteen, he was already publishing records in the *Entomologist*.[3] He read classics at Cambridge, went to Australia for a time as a teacher—his collections made there passing to the British Museum (Natural History)—and later taught classics at Kings School, Ely, and at Brentwood Grammar School.

Raynor is now mainly remembered as a collector and breeder of varieties of the magpie moth, *Abraxas grossulariata*. This conspicuous white moth, somewhat unpleasant to taste according to Ford,[4] spotted with black and streaked with yellow, is common in the Palaearctic and has an even wider distribution in picture galleries, for it is one of the ancillary subjects often introduced into still-life paintings by Jan Breughel the elder, Jan van Kessel, and other seventeenth-century artists of the

1. C. R. N. B[urrows]., Obituary, The Rev. Gilbert Henry Raynor, M.A., *Entom. Rec.*, *41*:139–40, 1929.

2. N. D. R[iley]., Rev. G. H. Raynor, *Entomologist*, *62*:239–40, 1929.

3. G. H. Raynor, Early appearance of *Platypteryx lacertula*, *Entomologist*, *5*:147, 1870.

4. E. B. Ford, Moths, *New Naturalist,* London, 1955.

Low Countries. Eleazar Albin, who was among the eighteenth-century Englishmen to continue the tradition of the artist-naturalist, dedicated Plate XLIII of *A Natural History of English Insects,* on which the moth is depicted, to Mrs. Bovey of Flaxley, but whether she had any other connection with *Abraxas grossulariata* is unelucidated.

The species is familiar in Britain wherever gooseberries and currants are cultivated, the larvae feeding on their leaves and sometimes being a pest. The adult is, in fact, often called the currant or gooseberry moth. As with many spotted insects, there is much variation in size and disposition of spots, some of which may run together, producing dark forms, or become obsolete, producing pale varieties. There are, in addition, three rather striking mutant genes, which have become of genetic interest and which produce in homozygous (or hemizygous) condition the aberrations *lutea, varleyata,* and *dohrnii* (Plate VI).

The first of these, widespread but uncommon in nature, has the whitish areas of the wing suffused with yellow; when heterozygous the *lutea* gene usually produces a yellow tinge to the front wings (ab. *semilutea*).

The second of these aberrations, *varleyata,* has black wings with a subbasal white stripe from costal to anal border. It was originally found by a Mr. J. Varley[5] of Huddersfield, who bred a specimen in 1864 that was figured on the frontispiece of the first volume of *The Naturalist,* published that year, a rather fuzzy color plate. Later he is said to have obtained ten more specimens that he sold at £1 apiece. The aberration was apparently not named till much later, by Raynor's "old friend" and frequent critic, G. T. Porritt, an amateur entomologist of great knowledge who did not hesitate to get involved with difficult groups such as the caddis flies. Ab. *varleyata* has occurred very sporadically in nature in Lancashire and South Yorkshire. Near Huddersfield, collections made by two working-

5. J. Varley, Remarkable varieties of *Abraxas grossulariata* and *Arctia caja, Naturalist, 1:*136–37, 1864.

men[6] gave, on one occasion, 15 specimens from 4,000 pupae collected, which, for an autosomal recessive, as *varleyata* proved to be, corresponds to a gene frequency of about 1 in 16 in the population sampled.

The third of the important aberrations, *dohrnii,* better known in the genetic literature by Raynor's later name *lacticolor,* and also named *deleta* by Cockerell and *flavofasciata* by Huene, occurs as a rare sporadic form in various parts of England and the continent of Europe, at least east to Estonia. All the wild-caught specimens are females. The black markings of ab. *dohrnii* are much reduced and the ground color of the wing has a creamy tint.[7] It was perhaps this form that was noted almost two hundred years ago (1764) at Enfield Chase by Drury, who records[8] a "Magpie (in the Eveng.) without any black spots on it scarcely an extraordinary odd Fly."

Raynor[9] started serious rearing of the magpie moth in 1899, obtaining many larvae from different parts of England. The study of variation by amateurs had become fashionable, partly under the influence of J. W. Tutt, who in his unfinished work on the British Lepidoptera attempted what was probably the most comprehensive and ambitious natural history of a group ever conceived. The first specimen of *dohrnii* to appear in Hazeleigh Rectory emerged on July 7, 1899, one of a large number of moths produced by larvae obtained from Lancashire.

6. G. T. Porritt, *Abraxas grossulariata var. varleyata* at Huddersfield, *Entom. Month. Mag., 41:*211, 1905.

7. Two forms, one due to a sex-linked recessive like *dohrnii,* reared by Poulton (see E. B. Ford, Problems of heredity in the Lepidoptera, *Biol. Rev., 12:*461–503, 1937), the other to an autosomal recessive (J. M. Woodlock, Some experiments in heredity with *Abraxas grossulariata* and two of its varieties, *J. Genetics, 5:*183–87, 1916) are known in which a comparable but less extreme reduction of black occurs; at least in Poulton's form the ground color was whitish rather than cream.

8. B. M. Hobby and E. B. Poulton, William Jones as a student of the British Lepidoptera, *Trans. Soc. Brit. Entom., 1:*149–55, 1934.

9. G. H. Raynor, Notes on *Abraxas grossulariata* and how to rear it, *Entom. Rec., 14:*321–25, 1902, *15:*8–11, 1903.

This specimen was mated to *grossulariata* and bred but, as we now would expect, its whole progeny was wild type. Fortunately, Raynor was not discouraged, and, breeding from these insects, obtained in 1901 rather over a score of the aberration, all females. When he published the account of his experiments late in the next year, all the specimens of the succeeding generation were wild type *grossulariata*. It must have been about this time he came to know Leonard Doncaster. As Bateson[10] wrote in his obituary of Doncaster, Raynor told the latter that all the specimens of the variety that he had bred were females. He also can hardly have avoided mentioning that his experience had indicated that the variety appeared in alternate generations. "At that time no example of what is now called 'sex-linked' inheritance amenable to experimentation had been studied. He [i.e. Doncaster] at once saw the extraordinary importance of the subject, and, as the result of correspondence with Mr. Raynor, matings were arranged and a critical investigation of the case was begun." The results, disclosing a "Mendelian recessive of quite a new type," were first made known[11] at an exhibit at the Cambridge meeting of the British Association for the Advancement of Science in 1904, and after more generations had been bred were described in a paper, "On Breeding Experiments with Lepidoptera," published in the *Proceedings* of the Zoological Society of London under joint authorship.[12] In this, two sets of experiments were reported, one of no great general importance, on *Angerona prunaria* "(experiments by L. Doncaster)," the other on *Abraxas grossulariata* "(experiments by the Rev. G. H. Raynor)." Raynor presented to the Zoological Museum of Cambridge University,

10. W. B[ateson]., Leonard Doncaster, 1877–1920, *Proc. R. Soc. London*, 92 B:xli–xlvi, 1921.

11. G. H. Raynor and L. Doncaster, Experiments on heredity and sex determination in *Abraxas grossulariata*, *Rep. Brit. Assoc. Adv. Sci. 1904* (Cambridge), pp. 594–95, 1905.

12. L. Doncaster and G. H. Raynor, Breeding experiments with Lepidoptera, *Proc. Zool. Soc. London*, 1906:1, pp. 125–33.

in the late summer or early autumn of 1907, "two cabinet drawers of *grossulariata* (chiefly ab. *lacticolor*), containing all the families that he had reared for heredity purposes and which were described by Mr. Doncaster and himself."[13] These specimens are still at Cambridge, with pedigrees and a suggested arrangement of the specimens written out by Doncaster. An ancestral pair of 1901, which were progenitors of most of the families studied, are included; the greater part of the material was bred in 1903 and 1904. Raynor therefore was certainly in touch with Doncaster between writing his account published late in 1902 and the breeding season of 1903.

In an obituary of Raynor by his friend the Reverend C. R. N. Burrows, it is suggested that part of Raynor's interest in the varieties of the Lepidoptera, and in particular of the magpie moth, was due to the recent rediscovery of Mendel's writings. It is, however, clear that he started work before this had happened. In none of his published notes or papers did he demonstrate any familiarity with genetic principles. He appeared more concerned with the beauty and strangeness of his specimens and with the extraordinary potentialities for variation that the species seemed to show. Moreover, at this time, as apparently earlier in his life, Raynor's entomological activities were not exclusively scientific and aesthetic, for, shortly after his munificent gift to the Zoological Museum at Cambridge, he put his collection up to auction,[14] realizing £487, of which nearly £200 came from 170 specially selected specimens of *A. grossulariata,* each provided with an aberrational name. Raynor's mentor and friend J. W. Tutt wrote of the Raynor sale.

> We never saw such a jam of "gooseberries" as at Stevens' room . . . when Mr. Raynor's collection was

13. [J. W. Tutt,] Current notes, *Entom. Rec., 19:*304, 1907.
14. C. R. N. Burrows, Sale of the "Raynor" Collection of Lepidoptera, *Entom. Rec., 19:*293–97, 1907.

sold. Nor were there wanting samples of the gooseberry fool, mellowed though they were by some of that cream, which regards these fine aberrations as matters of scientific interest and not, as so many say, postage stamps.[15]

Tutt felt that the sum realized was increased by the erroneous belief that some of the material was derived from the experiments done with Doncaster. The highest price of £6–10–0, was, however, paid for ab. *melanozona*, an aberration with fused spots forming a stripe across the fore wing, and for ab. *nigrolutea*, in which the fore wing is largely black and the pale ground color a fine yellow, rare and striking forms but not ones that had been the subject of any recorded genetic experiments. Higher prices, even allowing for inflation between 1907 and 1919, of up to 17½ guineas, were paid[16] in the latter year for nineteenth-century specimens of the completely white ab. *candida* Raynor, which, unlike his counterpart in John Moore's *The Fair Field*,[17] Raynor himself was never able to breed. Nor did he obtain the "pure black from which Mr. W. Beattie bred from Mickleham, and Mr. L. W. Newman from larvae of ab. *varleyata*. This I think may aptly be called ab. *nigra* n. ab. Should I be fortunate enough to rear either of these, I shall not say of *candida*, as Virgil did of horses 'color est deterrimus albis,' but in praise of *nigra*, I might be tempted to fire off the famous line 'Rara avis in terris, *nigroque* simillima cygno.' "[18]

15. Tutt (above, n. 13).
16. G. R. Raynor, A compendium of the named varieties of the large magpie moth *Abraxas grossulariata* with label list . . . obtainable only of the author, Hazeleigh Rectory, Maldon, Essex.
17. J. Moore, *The Fair Field*, New York, 1946.
18. G. H. Raynor, Further notes on *Abraxas grossulariata*, Entom. Rec., 21:270–72, 1909. The genetics of *nigra* are problematic and obviously peculiar; it may be an accentuated form of the black-dotted *nigrosparsata* (G. T. Porritt, Melanism in Abraxas grossulariata, *Entom. Month. Mag.*, 48:214, 1912; Abraxas grossulariata, var. nigra, *Entom. Month. Mag.*, 48:214, 1912; On the breeding of the variety nigrosparsata of Abraxas grossulariata, *Entom. Rec.*, 21:270–72, 1914). Porritt claimed that the specimen bred by

Sales of collections of Lepidoptera were an important feature of English natural history at the time; many specimens, including the two of *candida* (Dr. Kettlewell disagrees with Raynor's judgment on their appearance, in fact in them *color est deterrimus albis*) that passed, under Mr. Stevens' hammer, from one famous collection to another, must now have found a more abiding home in the great Rothschild-Cockayne-Kettlewell Collection at Tring. Sales of insect collections still occur, but the prices paid for varieties of *A. grossulariata* today are lower; two years ago a couple of ab. *nigra* fetched only five shillings.[19] The gooseberry fool seems rarer than at Raynor's sale in 1907 and is perhaps approaching extinction.

After the dispersal of his first collection of *A. grossulariata*, Raynor continued to breed the species almost till the end of his life, though accidents shortly before his death appear to have caused the loss of all his breeding stock. In his later years, from about 1916 onward, he became associated with the Hon. Huia Onslow, one of the most remarkable biologists of his time. Miss Croxon indicates that, in 1921, when Raynor retired, he went to live at Brampton in Huntingdonshire to be within easy distance of Cambridge, as he had many interests there. Foremost of these must have been Onslow and his experiments. Having injured his spine most seriously in a diving accident as an undergraduate, Onslow spent the remaining years of his life in a semirecumbent position. In spite of this

---

Newman is not comparable to the other known examples of *nigra* which have nothing to do with *varleyata*. Cockayne ("Gynandromorphism" and kindred problems, with descriptions and figures of some hitherto undescribed examples, *J. Genet.*, 5:75–131, 1915), figured a magnificent somatic mosaic, normal on the right, almost entirely black on the left without indication of the white basal stripes of *varleyata*, which suggests that a viable melanic mutant can occur independent of the latter. *Dohrnii*, perhaps *candida* and at least some of the more extreme, black forms are known from continental Europe.

19. C. G. M. de Wurms, The "Canon Watkinson" sale of Lepidoptera, *Entom. Rec.*, 92:22–24, 1963.

immense handicap he achieved during the span of his scientific career, of little less than a decade, an astonishing amount of work. He died at the age of 32, a year after Raynor retired to live nearer Cambridge. Onslow was one of the founders of biochemical genetics, and also left an extraordinary investigation of the iridescent colors of butterflies. The greater part of his work, however, concerns the genetics of color pattern in moths. In the first[20] of his seven papers on the subject, published in 1919, Onslow studied the yellow ab. *lutea* of *A. grossulariata*, proving, by an ingenious colorimetric method, that what looked like blending inheritance really involved Mendelian segregation. Again Raynor is standing in the background supplying breeding stock, information, and aberrational names. Onslow's pair of color plates illustrating the paper in fact provides the only published illustrations of some of Raynor's named aberrations. In the large pedigree that Onslow gives of his breeding experiments, the earlier part is due to Raynor, who clearly kept careful notes of the descent of his specimens, even though his published remarks give the impression of quite unsystematic breeding. It is certainly incorrect to suggest, as Burrows did in his obituary, that there was no written record; rather it seems that it was destroyed posthumously (Cockayne *fide* Kettlewell, personal information). Onslow's work in turn led on to that of Ford,[21] who demonstrated that the incomplete dominance expressed in *semilutea* could be greatly modified in either direction by selection, so that whether the yellow color was dominant or recessive depended on the genetic constitution of the animal under observation. Onslow,[22] in a later paper, returned to *A. grossulariata*, working this time with the

20. H. Onslow, The inheritance of wing colour in Lepidoptera: *I, Abraxas grossulariata* var. *lutea* (Cockerell), *J. Genet., 8*:209–58, 1919.

21. E. B. Ford, Genetic research in the Lepidoptera, *Ann. Eugen., 10*:227–52, 1940.

22. H. Onslow, The inheritance of wing colour in Lepidoptera: *V*, Melanism in *Abraxas grossulariata* (var. *varleyata* Porritt), *J. Genet., 11*:123–39, 1921.

melanic *varleyata,* obtained in part from Raynor, in part from G. T. Porritt. Onslow found *varleyata* to depend on an autosomal recessive gene, as was indeed fairly clear from the anecdotal data of the earlier breeders. He also studied a number of modifications of the *varleyata* pattern, including ab. *actinota* Raynor, which seems to involve a peculiar type of perhaps sex-limited inheritance confined to the male, and ab. *exquisita* Raynor, which appears to be the expression of homozygous *varleyata* in an individual that would otherwise be phenotypically *dohrnii.*[23] Raynor, with his customary abstention from genetic interpretation, merely indicates that certain yellow forms derived from *dohrnii* had been crossed with *varleyata* in producing *exquisita;* he is more interested in expatiating on the beauties of what to the nonconnoisseur would look like an unfamiliar but by no means extraordinary insect. Onslow promised a further analysis of *exquisita,* but died before it was completed.

Though Onslow's work on *A. grossulariata* produced nothing as fundamental as sex-linked inheritance, the studies on ab. *lutea* are of considerable theoretical importance as a remarkable early example of the Mendelian analysis of apparent blending inheritance. As with Doncaster, so with Onslow, it was Raynor's breeding experience which made the work possible. In the case of Doncaster's work, the results represented an immense contribution to the study of heredity, which contribution led toward the chromosomal theory developed in America in the next decade, and so to all that has happened subsequently in genetics. Raynor's skill in breeding and his obvious delight in the protean beauty of the magpie moth lie behind this and so are one of the small roots of modern science—*exaltavit humiles.*[24]

23. E. B. Ford, Problems of heredity in the Lepidoptera, *Biol. Rev.,* 12:461–503, 1937: see also above, n. 4.

24. Apart from my very great debt to Miss Croxon and the Reverend C. G. Bartle, I should like also to express my thanks to H. B. D. Kettlewell of Oxford, John Smart of Cambridge, and C. R. Remington of Yale University, who have helped in various ways in the preparation of this account.

Index

Systematic Index of Organisms

Authors' names are given for species and infraspecific taxa, followed by the English name (capital initial) or other indication of the kind of plant or animal

Abraxas grossulariata (Linnaeus): Large Magpie, Currant or Gooseberry Moth, 122–30, Pl. vi; ab. *actinota* Raynor, 130, Pl. vi; ab. *albipalliata* Raynor, Pl. vi; ab. *candida* Raynor, 127–28; ab. *centralipunctata* Raynor, Pl. vi; ab. *dohrnii* Koenig (=*flavofasciata* Huene, *deleta* Cockerell, *lacticolor* Raynor), 123–24, Pl. vi; ab. *exquisita* Raynor, 130, Pl. vi; ab. *flavipalliata* Raynor, Pl. vi; ab. *fulvapicata* Raynor, Pl. vi; ab. *hazeleighensis* Raynor, Pl. vi; ab. *leucosticta* Raynor, Pl. vi; ab. *lutea* Cockerell, 123, 129, Pl. vi; ab. *melanozona* Raynor, 127; ab. *nigra* Raynor, 127–28; ab. *nigrolutea* Raynor, 127; ab. *nigrosparsata* Raynor, Pl. vi; ab. *nigrovarleyata* Porritt, Pl. vi; ab. *pulchra* Raynor, Pl. vi; ab. *semilutea* Raynor, 123; ab. *varleyata* Porritt, 123, 127, 128n, 129n, 130, Pl. vi

Acyrthosiphon pisum (Harris): aphid, 57

Anacystis: blue-green alga, 111–12

Angerona prunaria (Linnaeus): Orange Moth, 125

Anisops: back-swimmer, 53–55, 59; *A. bouvieri* Kirkaldy, 53–54; *A. debilis* Gerstaecker, 59; *A. elegans* Fieber (=*apicalis* Stål), 60; *A. extendofrons* Brooks, 53–54; *A. gracilis* Hutchinson, 59; *A. jaczewskii* Hutchinson, 59; *A. madagascarensis* Poisson, 54–55; *A. pellucens* Gerstaecker, 60; *A. praetexta* Hutchinson, 59; *A. sardea* Herrick-Schaeffer, 54, 59; *A. varia scutellata* Fieber, 59

Anser indicus Latham: Bar-headed Goose, 2

Anthocoris: Flower Bug, 56–57; *A. gallarum-ulmi* (De Geer): Elm Gall Flower Bug, 57; *A. sarothamni* Douglas and Scott: Broom Flower Bug, 57; *A. visci* Douglas: Mistletoe Flower Bug, 57

Aquila verrauxi Lesson: Verreaux's Eagle, 72; *A. wahlbergi* Sundevall: Wahlberg's Eagle, 72–73

Arctia caja (Linnaeus): Common Tiger Moth, 123n

Arenaria muscosa Med.: Sandwort, 4

Artemisia minor Jacq.: mugwort, 6n

Arytaina genistae (Latreille): psyllid, 57

Asplanchna: rotifer, 117

Baltia: pierid or white butterfly, 6

Bramapithecus thorpei. See *Ramapithecus*

Brontosaurus: dinosaur, 26

General Index